SOLAR THROAT
SLASHED

WESLEYAN POETRY

AIMÉ CÉSAIRE

SOLAR THROAT SLASHED

THE UNEXPURGATED 1948 EDITION

TRANSLATED AND EDITED BY
A. James Arnold and Clayton Eshleman

WESLEYAN UNIVERSITY PRESS
Middletown, Connecticut

Wesleyan University Press
Middletown CT 06459
www.wesleyan.edu/wespress
© 2011 by A. James Arnold and Clayton Eshleman
All rights reserved
Manufactured in the United States of America

Wesleyan University Press is a member of the Green
Press Initiative. The paper used in this book meets their
minimum requirement for recycled paper.

Library of Congress Cataloging-in-Publication Data
appear on the last printed page of this book.

5 4 3 2 1

Cet ouvrage a bénéficié du soutien des Programmes
d'aide à la publication de Culturesfrance/Ministère
français des affaires étrangères et européennes.

This work, published as part of a program of aid for
publication, received support from CulturesFrance and
the French Ministry of Foreign Affairs.

 This project is supported in part by an award
from the National Endowment for the Arts

CONTENTS

Introduction xi

Magique 2
La parole aux oricous 4
Lynch I 6
Dévoreur 8
La loi est nue 10
La pluie 12
Allure 14
Désastre 16
Société secrète 18
Traversée nocturne 20
Entre autres massacres 22
Le griffon 24
Rachat 26
Mississipi 28
Blues 30
Le bouc émissaire 32
Transmutation 34
Demeure I 36
Le coup de couteau du soleil dans le dos des villes surprises 38
À l'heure où dans la chaleur les moines descendent de l'Himalaya 40
Attentat aux mœurs 42
Fils de la Foudre 44
Laissez-passer 46
Solide 48
La femme et la flamme 50
Millibars de l'orage 52
Galanterie de l'histoire 54
À quelques milles de la surface 56
Chevelure 58
Scalp 62
La tornade 64
Lynch II 66
Apothéose 68
Croisade du Silence 70
Totem 72
Défaire et refaire le soleil 74
Samba 78
Intercesseur 80
La roue 82

Magic 3
The Nubian Vultures Have the Floor 5
Lynch I 7
Devourer 9
The Law is Naked 11
Rain 13
Velocity 15
Disaster 17
Secret Society 19
Nocturnal Crossing 21
Among Other Massacres 23
The Griffin 25
Redemption 27
Mississippi 29
Blues 31
The Scapegoat 33
Transmutation 35
Dwelling I 37
The Sun's Knife-Stab in the Back of the Surprised Cities 39
When in the Heat of the Day Naked Monks Descend the Himalayas 41
Attack on Morals 43
Son of Thunder 45
Permit 47
Solid 49
The Woman and the Flame 51
Millibars of the Storm 53
Gallantry of History 55
Several Miles from the Surface 57
Chevelure 59
Scalp 63
The Tornado 65
Lynch II 67
Apotheosis 69
Crusade of Silence 71
Totem 73
Unmaking and Remaking the Sun 75
Samba 79
Intercessor 81
The Wheel 83

Calme 84
An neuf 86
Ex-voto pour un naufrage 88
Depuis Akkad depuis Élam depuis Sumer 92
Au serpent 94
Torture 98
Fanion 100
À l'Afrique 102
Délicatesse d'une momie 106
Démons 108
Marais 110
Couteaux-Midi 112
Idylle 116
Mot de passe 120
Tournure des choses 122
Question préalable 124
Tatouage des regards 126
Aux écluses du vide 128
Déshérence 132
À la nuit 136
Quelconque 138
Ode à la Guinée 142
Cheval 146
Demeure antipode 150
Soleil et eau 154
D'une métamorphose 156
Marche des perturbations 158
Barbare 160
Cercle non vicieux 162
Autre horizon 164
Mort à l'aube 166
À hurler 168
Jugement de la lumière 170

Calm 85
New Year 87
Ex-Voto for a Shipwreck 89
All the Way from Akkad, from Elam, from Sumer 93
To the Serpent 95
Torture 99
Pennant 101
To Africa 103
Delicacy of a Mummy 107
Demons 109
Swamp 111
Noon Knives 113
Idyll 117
Password 121
Turn of Events 123
Preliminary Question 125
Tattooing Gazes 127
At the Locks of the Void 129
Forfeiture 133
To the Night 137
Commonplace 139
Ode to Guinea 143
Horse 147
Antipodal Dwelling 151
Sun and Water 155
From a Metamorphosis 157
March of Perturbations 159
Barbarity 161
Non-Vicious Circle 163
Different Horizon 165
Death at Dawn 167
Howling 169
The Light's Judgment 171

Notes 173
Acknowledgments 183
About the Authors 185

INTRODUCTION

Aimé Césaire emerged as a powerful new voice in French poetry between 1946 and 1948. Gallimard, which had rapidly become the premier literary publisher in French after World War I, issued his first collection, entitled The Miraculous Weapons (Les Armes miraculeuses), one year after the end of World War II. A number of poems had previously appeared in the Martinique journal Tropiques and in the New York magazines VVV and Hémisphères during the war. The Miraculous Weapons revealed the bold experimentation of the Martinican poet, then thirty-three years of age and completely unknown. The following year André Breton prefaced the first Paris edition of Césaire's long poem Notebook of a Return to the Native Land (Cahier d'un retour au pays natal), which had been published in Spanish translation in Havana in 1942 and in a bilingual edition in New York earlier in 1947. Although quite different from one another, the two 1947 editions of Notebook share a marked surrealist inflection in the use of metaphor and theme that Césaire would edit out of the poem in 1956. Soleil cou coupé (Solar Throat Slashed) was published in 1948 by a publisher known only as "K" who specialized in challenging new work. Soleil cou coupé had a press run of 2,160 copies, 60 of which the German surrealist Hans Hartung illustrated with original engravings. That same year K published Antonin Artaud's polemical radio poem Pour en finir avec le jugement de Dieu (To Have Done With The Judgment Of God). Soleil cou coupé was the capstone of a series of three major works marked by a revolutionary new poetics.

Readers of the present edition will be able for the first time to properly appreciate Césaire's poetic accomplishment just before midcentury, at a time when he maintained his friendships among the Paris Surrealists while serving in the French Chamber of Deputies as a Communist representative from Martinique. These were years of severe frustration and disappointment for the legislator who had cosponsored the law that turned the Old Colonies—Martinique, Guadeloupe (in the West Indies), French Guyane (on the Caribbean coast of South America), and Réunion Island in the Indian Ocean—into overseas departments or DOMs (Départements d'Outre-Mer) in 1946–47. The government in Paris had procrastinated on implementing the new status; the modernization of Martinique's infrastructure, which as mayor of Fort-de-France Césaire was eager to push forward, seemed to recede into the future.

The Cold War had not yet broken out in earnest; the political poetry published in the collection Ferrements (Ferraments), 1960 (1983), had yet to be written. Direct criticism of U.S. foreign policy of the sort one finds in many of the best-known poems of Ferrements is absent; but derisive condemnation of Jim Crow and racial segregation stand behind the irony in such poems as "Tornado" and "Mississipi." Europe, too, comes in for some severe bashing by Césaire, notably in the conclusion of "At the Locks of the Void." Césaire had seen the hope of a left-of-center political revival in France and its overseas possessions dashed as the country rallied around Gaullist nationalism and the preservation of the French colonial empire in the immediate postwar period.

Readers who bring a postcolonial mindset to Césaire's poetry in Solar Throat Slashed may feel disconcerted at first. The "Africa" we find in this collection is a mental construction that gestures toward the "arbitrary lands" of "Ode to Guinea," the "shipwrecks" of "Attack on Morals" and "Chevelure," and the "disasters" of "Ex-Voto for a Shipwreck" and "Commonplace." Taken together, these images allude to the desolate moral climate of colonialism, one of "Forfeiture" or "Disaster." It is a climate of tropical diseases of every description that "Chevelure" sums up as "plague." If the Caribbean, the French West Indies, and, indeed, Martinique itself remain unnamed in these poems, Africa is represented as a largely undifferentiated region, both ancestral home and origin in a precolonial past. The occasional Bedouin or Carib who makes a fleeting appearance does not seem connected to a real place in the contemporary world. Exceptionally the name of a historical figure gives a semblance of specificity to the poems. Both Shaka ("Ex-Voto for a Shipwreck") and Almamy Samory ("Pennant") were military heroes and precolonial empire builders. The role they play in the collection, however, is more emblematic than historical. Even the "peasant" of "To Africa" is an emblematic figure, striking the soil with his pick hoe in a gesture that is more magical than agricultural in its repetitive penetration of the maternal earth. Who then are the inhabitants of this Africa that is both disinherited and mythic?

*

The representation of Africa in this collection is directly related to the internal contradictions of negritude, which emerge each time the word nègre is encountered in a different context. Meaning in poetry is contextual; every translation is also and inescapably an interpretation. Translators' choices are the result of careful attention to both internal context (the poem's dynamics) and tone. In our work on Solar Throat Slashed the dictates of political correctness never impinged on interpretation of what Césaire was about in 1948, writing as he was in a climate far removed from the strictures imposed on language and ethnicity in the United States more than a half-century later. Jacqueline Couti, a young Martinican scholar who has written on language, ethnicity, and sexuality in contemporary Martinique, was very helpful in handling these issues. How could one avoid translating as "niggers" the "massacred niggers or redskins" in "Disaster"? The deprecatory context renders every other choice meaningless. In "Tornado," which is set in a stereotyped southern U.S. town, the phrase "stinking like ten thousand niggers crammed into a train" called for the same solution to render racist violence. In "Idyll" the translation "like a house nigger bearing agile milk" would have called for "Negro" a half-century ago in the United States. Today the same translation would lose the expressive condemnation contained in Césaire's use of *nègre*. In "To Africa," however, the praise for the peasant laborer contained in the lines "for you have neither the glistening strength of the buffalo nor the mathematical science of the ibis nor the patience of the black man" called for a respectful term to represent the architect of Africa's future. In "Noon Knives" the French line "Quand les Nègres font la Révolution" was more troublesome. At the outset Césaire takes a mythological approach to revolution that represents something like a struggle among the gods of Olympus; then he proceeds to play satirically on terms representing "black" and "white" as racial antagonists. The translation finally came down on the side of "the Blacks," capitalized exceptionally as was "Nègres" in the original. The translators trust readers to take these linguistic signs as markers of the poet's intent at a specific point in a given poem rather than as rigidly fixed units containing their own, presumably immutable, meaning.

★

Readers of Clayton Eshleman's and Annette Smith's translation of Césaire's *Collected Poetry* (University of California Press, 1983) may be in for a shock. The text of *Solar Throat Slashed* they translated lacked just over 40 percent of the original poems, whereas many of the remaining titles had been more or less severely edited to bring them into line with the political aims of the blended collection *Cadastre* (1961), which coincided with the first flush of excitement over independence in Africa. The University of California Press edition was bound by the conditions that the revised text imposed on individual poems as well as on the collection as a whole. Consequently, the modernist poetry Césaire had practiced throughout the 1940s, and which reached its full fruition in the 1948 edition of *Soleil cou coupé*, was substantially obliterated. It therefore seemed to us urgent to restore to his memory, and to his stature as a great twentieth-century poet, this important collection that antedates by nearly a decade the political turn that caused Césaire to censor his earlier poetics, beginning in 1956 with the so-called definitive edition of the Notebook. The Wesleyan University Press bilingual edition of Solar Throat Slashed reestablishes the collection's original integrity. The previously translated poems that appeared under the part title "Cadastre" in Collected Poetry have been reviewed by Clayton Eshleman and myself and modified wherever the radical originality of the complete collection called for retranslation.

In 1948 Soleil cou coupé had a broadly magico-religious frame of reference that Césaire either edited out or minimized in the revised collection published in Cadastre ("land registry"). Indeed, there is a fundamental shift of vision between the 1948 and 1961 editions. In order to realign his collection with a political position consonant with the immediate postcolonial period, especially with regard to African independence, Césaire simply dropped the great majority of the poems that are permeated by magical, religious, and sexual imagery. The prophetic stance of the poetic "I" in 1948 is minimized through the same process and replaced with a more politically committed posture. The self-censorship that presided over the revision of Soleil cou coupé can be found in the post-1956 editions of all the major poetic texts written in the 1940s. The tragic oratorio And the Dogs Were Silent, first published as a constitutive part of The Miraculous Weapons in 1946, becomes the Brechtian satire issued in 1956 as a theatrical text by Présence Africaine. The surrealist tenor of the two 1947 editions of Notebook of a Return to the Native Land is replaced in the 1956 Présence Africaine edition by new passages detailing the exploitation of labor in Martinique. Consequently, readers who have had access only to these heavily revised editions can have no familiarity with, and what is more serious for Césaire's reputation, no expectation of the poet's radical originality in the original edition of Soleil cou coupé.

Césaire's practice of free associative metaphor (métaphore filée), which is most often identified with surrealist poetry, was minimized by cutting single lines and long passages of poems that in 1961 take on a character quite different from the poetics of the 1948 edition. Consequently, both his poetic practice and the overall orientation of the collection underwent a sea change between 1948 and 1961. The challenge to the translators has been to find ways to restore as much as possible of the apparently wild and free associative imagery of the 1948 Soleil cou coupé. I stress the adverb "apparently." The wildness and the sense of utter freedom the reader initially takes away from the poems derive, in large measure, from the poems' refusal to respond to reader expectations. Efforts to grasp the meaning of each word taken individually or in a single syntactic unit are thwarted by Césaire's poetics, which proceeds in strings of imagery, sometimes short, sometimes quite long, that nonetheless maintain a fairly clear syntactic relationship. (The word logic would be too restrictive here since it introduces the faculty of reason that Césaire intends to short-circuit.)

Our translation process, which has sometimes generated as many as ten versions of a particularly complex poem, has involved accommodating the freer syntactic linking of phrases and clauses in English to the more rigid syntax of French. Thus, both the relative pronoun "that" and the prepositions "of" and "by" occur more frequently here than is common in similarly innovative American poetry. These tool words are markers of Césaire's practice of juxtaposition or parataxis in parallel relative clauses and in compound prepositional phrases that express agency or belonging. Anaphora—the repetition of a word or phrase in the initial position in a line of poetry—is as important to Césaire's grammar in *Solar Throat Slashed* as it was in his *Notebook of a Return to the Native Land*. Admiring readers of Césaire's long poem, especially in Africa, have seen in his systematic use of anaphora a sign of African inspiration because of the importance of this poetic turn in ritual texts and epic poetry. There is, however, no evidence that Césaire was familiar with African oral texts in the 1940s. His use of anaphora to drive home a point while short-circuiting rational critique is very close to the practice of Charles Péguy, the socialist poet who enjoyed a position of preeminence among left-wing Catholics in pre–World War I France. In later years Césaire seems never to have mentioned Péguy among his formative influences, no doubt to distance himself from the right-wing colonialist positions of the Catholic hierarchy, but it is significant that he published a celebratory article on Péguy in the newspaper *Action Socialiste* in late October 1939, immediately following his return from France.

Among the French poets of the interwar period with whom Césaire struggles in order to find and affirm his own original voice, one must mention Paul Claudel and Saint-John Perse, both of whom perfected in the twentieth century the liberation of French poetry from a restrictive set of rules inherited from the seventeenth. Césaire sometimes specified that he was attracted to Claudel, prior to the French poet's reconversion to Catholicism, for the Nietzschean tragic poetics he found in the early plays. As for Saint-John Perse, he remains a bone of contention for many French West Indians. Perse was the scion of a ruined planter family who was born in Guadeloupe and rose to a very high position in the French civil service before World War II. He was stripped of his citizenship by the Nazis during the Occupation, served as a poetry consultant at the Library of Congress during the war, and received the Nobel Prize for Literature in 1960. A careful contrastive analysis of his poetry with Césaire's would require a long essay. Suffice it to say here that Perse's evocation of the Guadeloupe of his early childhood is characterized by his intense vision of an idyllic landscape and the fixed hierarchy of people within their rigidly prescribed ethnoclass roles. His long, dense poetic line is dominated by noun clauses that ascribe a cosmic permanence to the plantation social order into which Perse was born. Césaire's vision of the natural world is as intense and as precise as Perse's, but there the positive comparison ends. Césaire's "To the Serpent" can be read as an anti-edenic poem in which the Judeo-Christian vision of creation is countered by reverential address to the wily serpent who tempts the biblical Eve. The crow in this poem takes us to "Idyll," a poem in which all of nature seems to be entangled with this bird of ill omen. Césaire's poetic line, while frequently as hermetic as Perse's, is dominated by verbs and active participial and gerundive forms. It is a world in a state of incredible tension, relieved sporadically by some cataclysmic event. Césaire's free associative metaphors frequently look backward and forward in the line simultaneously, obliging the translator to make painful choices as to both function and meaning. But in the poem "Preliminary Question" we see the speaker humorously praising the process of metaphoric transformation itself for its salvatory properties:

> I piss a camel bearing a pope and vanish in a row of fig trees that quite neatly encircle the intruder and strangle him in a beautiful tropical balancing act

For a brief moment the poet thumbs his nose at the tortures imposed by the colonial system and glories in his status as a tropical Prometheus.

Although Césaire took care to distinguish himself from the French Surrealists, it was unquestionably André Breton who championed the Martinican poet's early career. Breton's "A Great Negro Poet," which introduced the New York bilingual edition of *Return to My Native Land*—the title of the *Notebook* in the translation by Lionel Abel and Yvan Goll for Brentano's in 1947—was for some time the most extensive presentation of Césaire's poetry in English. Breton also laid the groundwork for the notion, propounded by Jean-Paul Sartre in 1948, that Césaire was a "Black Orpheus" whose vision constituted the antidote to the ideology of the colonial world. However, the internal contradiction, extreme tension, and complexity in Césaire's imagery place him closer to the late poetry of Artaud than to Breton. Scores of electroshock sessions left Artaud with an immediacy of anguished vision that one rarely senses in Breton. No doubt Césaire doesn't take us nearly as far into the mental maelstrom, but he does open up perspectives that are sometimes dizzying and disconcerting. The French poets who were common ancestors to both the Surrealists and Césaire include Lautréamont, Rimbaud, and Mallarmé as well. Césaire wrote illuminating essays on Lautréamont and Mallarmé for the cultural magazine *Tropiques*, which he co-edited with fellow secondary school teachers (including his wife, Suzanne) in Fort-de-France between 1941 and 1945. Césaire found in Lautréamont a bold freedom in the creation of images, which Breton himself had pointed to as models of surrealist metaphor. In "Several Miles from the

Surface" the incongruous image of "the long coitus of a tree with a sailboat" exemplifies this type of metaphor. In Mallarmé he found a syntax that utterly destroyed the vaunted clarity and the rational basis of poetry written in French, thereby authorizing the Martinican poet to challenge the authority of the colonial system through its very language. Rimbaud was for Césaire, as he most certainly was for Breton, the visionary whose poetry opened up vistas previously unimaginable in French. Apollinaire occupies a privileged place in the conception and creation of *Solar Throat Slashed*, which borrows its title from the final lines of his poem "Zone." Among early twentieth-century French poets, Apollinaire stands out for his blending of a spiritual yearning, an extraordinary openness to the arts of the colonized world (then thought of as "primitive"), and an unusually free erotic imagination. Césaire was to combine all these elements in new and unexpected ways in *Solar Throat Slashed*.

The pervasive element in *Solar Throat Slashed* that may appear most surprising to those who know Césaire's poetry only from versions that had as their starting point the heavily revised *Notebook of a Return to the Native Land* in 1956 is the religious imagery and the pervasive climate of spirituality. Césaire alludes to Vodun in "Gallantry of History," "All the Way from Akkad, from Elam, from Sumer," and "March of Perturbations." He blasphemes against Christianity and its complicity with colonialism in "To Africa," "Noon Knives," and "From a Metamorphosis," referring to "the commandant's God" in "All the Way from Akkad, from Elam, from Sumer." In the poem "Calm" he invokes the "towers of silence" on which the Zoroastrians exposed their dead; and in "To Africa" he alludes to the Babylonian divinity Ishtar. The speaker in the poem not infrequently adopts a prayerful rhetoric that relies heavily on anaphoric devices suggestive of litany. In at least two instances ("To Africa" and "Blues") Césaire invokes the Babylonian captivity, thus assimilating the dispersion of the African diaspora to the destruction of the kingdom of Judah by Nebuchadnezzar. "Blues" is Césaire's modernist turn on Psalm 137 ("By the waters of Babylon, there we sat down, yea, we wept, when we remembered Zion"). Sometimes the reader can, as is the case in "Blues," seize the spiritual intertext so as to gain a culturally informed sense of the direction in which the poem intends to take us. In my 1981 study of Césaire's poetry, *Modernism and Negritude* (193–98), I gave an extended example of his reliance on the biblical book of Revelation (in French *l'Apocalypse*) so as to link images in the poem "The Sun's Knife-Stab in the Back of the Surprised Cities" to an apocalyptic vision of renewal. Poems of this type were systematically eliminated from the 1961 reframing of the collection for *Cadastre*. They remained lost to Césaire's body of work until publication of the present bilingual edition.

The type of metaphor that André Breton described as exploding-fixed is particularly well suited to Césaire's poetic persona. Rather than resolving the tension between elements brought into unexpected contact in his strings of associative metaphors, the exploding-fixed type bursts like fireworks from the accumulation of its strange, contradictory elements. The result is a numinous revelation of we know not what, unknown and perhaps unknowable, that nonetheless promises renewal and transformation:

> and how I do love the circulation of the blood of disaster
> in the veins of a ten-storied house at the sublime moment preceding
> its collapse at the stroke of 3 P.M. ("Several Miles from the Surface")

and in the conclusion to "Unmaking and Remaking the Sun":

> Dwelling made of your impotence of the power of my simple acts of the
> freedom of my spermatozoa dwelling black womb hung with a red curtain
> sole altar I may bless while watching the world explode at the option of
> my silence

This is the "magic" promised by the liminary poem of *Solar Throat Slashed*. All these poetic devices, which delve deeply into a shared cultural memory, serve a transcendent, apocalyptic vision. A solar divinity presides over this collection, appearing at crucial junctures ("Among Other Massacres," "Transmutation," "The Sun's Knife-Stab in the Back of the Surprised Cities," "Unmaking and Remaking the Sun") to provide a loose structuring device that suggests a narrative of creation, destruction and recreation. As the speaker says in "At the Locks of the Void":

> It is I who sing with a voice still caught up in the babbling of elements. It is
> sweet to be a piece of wood a cork a drop of water in the torrential waters
> of the end and of the new beginning. It is sweet to doze off in the shattered
> heart of things.

Césaire's transformative vision is most often violent, but not revolutionary in any political sense. Indeed there is nothing at all like a political process expressed, invoked or alluded to in this collection. In "Ode to Guinea" the sun is assimilated to "Guinée" itself (the mythic home of descendants of slaves in the French- and Creole-speaking Caribbean), to which the poetic prayer or supplication is addressed. The role of woman as telluric force in this poem—she is assimilated to the mountain, the earth, and fire—is typical of Césaire's vision. He imagines the eventual transformation of the colonial order as catastrophic. The synecdoche of this apocalyptic transformation is the volcano, whose eruptive, ejaculatory violence is for Césaire the ultimate gesture of masculinity. Since Césaire later in his career described himself to journalists as a Pelean personality, just as vulcanologists speak of the Pelean type of explosion, he has invited readers to see in the explosive violence of many of these poems an image of Mt. Pelée, which destroyed the old colonial capital of Martinique in May 1902. To reduce the solar and volcanic imagery in Solar Throat Slashed to a discrete historic event, however, is to misunderstand the poetic process that informs the collection.

In its broadest outline Solar Throat Slashed presents elements of a cosmogonic myth. The solar divinity is finally self-immolating, promising renewal through the process of destruction and recreation. The first published version of And the Dogs Were Silent (1946) presented an agonistic tragic hero, the Rebel, who suffers, is humiliated, and is murdered for the ultimate transformation of the colonized world. While researching my introduction to Eshleman and Smith's translation of a late version of this play, published in 1990 with i, laminaria . . . under the title Lyric and Dramatic Poetry (1946–1982), I realized that certain images of death and transfiguration in And the Dogs Were Silent pointed to the myth of Isis and Osiris in the Egyptian Book of the Dead, as well as to Frazer's Golden Bough (Césaire, Lyric and Dramatic Poetry, xxi, n. 16). Césaire has disseminated many of these same elements throughout Solar Throat Slashed, and especially the privileged relationship of the poetic "I" to the sun. His borrowing of the title from Apollinaire points to the sacrifice of the solar divinity to a cosmic process that Césaire presents as an alternative spiritual principle. He systematically discredits Christianity as the handmaiden of colonization, while appealing to any number of pre-Christian religious systems as more appropriate to the needs of the colonized world. The poem "Intercessor" provides the reader with a dense synecdoche of this process:

"O torn sun
  blind peacock magical and cool
  with arched test tube hands
  futile eclipse of space"

We can read the conclusion of this poem, in the context of the collection as a whole, as a prayer to the sun god who was "torn" in the slashing of his throat, who remains magical and splendid ("peacock") although blinded (like Oedipus?), and who is mysteriously associated with the "eclipse" of space. In the final metaphoric turn, the eclipse of the sun and the "eclipse" of space in colonized Africa become one. On this reading of the solar imagery that provides the linking and binding elements of the collection, "The Light's Judgment" becomes Césaire's answer to the Last Judgment of the colonial, Christian world. As the final numinous word of Solar Throat Slashed, the "victorious sun" promises "justice" and "upright judgment" that will dismiss "all arrogance."

In his notes on the poem "Noon Knives," Clayton Eshleman recommends an article by Janice Horner Kaufman, who demonstrates in detail the extent to which Césaire relied upon the German ethnographer Frobenius's now-discredited concept of cultural transformation in Africa. Césaire followed Frobenius closely in interpreting the "Ethiopian" culture of colonized black Africans and their cousins in the diaspora as virile but plantlike. Many of the poems in this collection work out just such a dynamic. As Césaire suggests in "Millibars of the Storm," the purpose of his poetry in Solar Throat Slashed is "to liberate the space where bristles the heart of things and the advent of man." His ultimate goal in this collection is, in the broadest sense, spiritual. After the apocalyptic cataclysm, after transformation and metamorphosis, humankind will have realized the promise of the "New Year": ". . . when the seeds of humankind chose within man the tender path of a new heart."

AJA
Staunton, Virginia
March–June 2010

SOLAR THROAT SLASHED

Magique

avec une lèche de ciel sur un quignon de terre
vous bêtes qui sifflez sur le visage de cette morte
vous libres fougères parmi les roches assassines
à l'extrême de l'île parmi les conques trop vastes pour leur destin
lorsque midi colle ses mauvais timbres sur les plis tempétueux de la louve
hors cadre de science nulle
et la bouche aux parois du nid suffète des îles englouties comme un sou

avec une lèche de ciel sur un quignon de terre
prophète des îles oubliées comme un sou
sans sommeil sans veille sans doigt sans palancre
quand la tornade passe rongeur du pain des cases

vous bêtes qui sifflez sur le visage de cette morte
la belle once de la luxure et la coquille operculée
mol glissement des grains de l'été que nous fûmes
belles chairs à transpercer du trident des aras
lorsque les étoiles chancelières de cinq branches
trèfles au ciel comme des gouttes de lait chu
réajustent un dieu noir mal né de son tonnerre

Magic

with a thin slice of sky on a hunk of earth
you beasts hissing into the face of this dead woman
you ferns free amidst the murderous rocks
at the far point of the island amidst conches too vast for their destiny
when noon sticks its wicked stamps on the tempestuous folds of the she-wolf
beyond the pale of worthless science
and plugs her against the walls of the nest suffete of the islands swallowed up
like a sou

with a thin slice of sky on a hunk of earth
prophet of the islands forgotten like a sou
without sleep without vigil without a finger without a trawl
when the tornado passes gnawer at the bread of the huts

you beasts hissing into the face of this dead woman
the beautiful snow leopard of lust and the operculated shell
languid glide of the summer grain that we were
beautiful flesh to be pierced by the macaws' trident
when the five-branched chancelloress stars
clover in the sky like drops of fallen milk
reinstate a black god ill-born of his thunder

La parole aux oricous

Où quand comment d'où pourquoi oui pourquoi pourquoi pourquoi se peut-il que les langues les plus scélérates n'aient inventé que si peu de crocs à pendre ou suspendre le destin ses pompes et ses aisselles

Arrêtez cet homme innocent. Tous de leurre. Il porte mon sang sur les épaules. Il porte mon sang dans ses souliers. Il colporte mon sang dans son nez. Mort aux contrebandiers. Les frontières sont fermées. Quelle horrible cocaïne. Ni pouce ni police. Que la mort soit immédiate. Ni su ni insu tous
dieu merci mon cœur est plus sec que l'harmattan, toute obscurité m'est proie
toute obscurité m'est due, et toute bombe joie.

Vous oricous à vos postes de tournoiement et de bec au-dessus de la forêt et jusqu'à la caverne dont la porte est un triangle
dont le gardien est un chien
dont la vie est un calice
dont la vierge est une araignée
dont le sillage rare est un lac à se mettre debout sur les chemins de déchant des nixes orageuses

The Nubian Vultures Have the Floor

Where when how from whence why yes why why why is it that the most villainous tongues have invented so few hooks on which to hang or suspend destiny its pomp and its armpits

Arrest this innocent man. All decoys. He carries my blood on his shoulders. He carries my blood in his shoes. Peddles my blood in his nose. Death to the smugglers. The borders are closed. What horrible cocaine. Neither thumb nor screw. Let death be instantaneous. Neither known nor unknown
all
thank god my heart is drier than the harmattan, all darkness is my prey all darkness is my due, and every burst joy.

You Nubian vultures at your hovering and pecking stations over the forest and as far as the cavern whose door is a triangle
whose guardian is a dog
whose life is a chalice
whose virgin is a spider
whose rare wake is a lake for standing upright on the descant roads of stormy nixies

Lynch I

Pourquoi le printemps me prend-il à la gorge? que me veut-il? et quand bien même il n'aurait pas assez de lances et de fanions! Je te conspue printemps d'afficher ton œil borgne et ton haleine mauvaise. Ton stupre tes baisers infâmes. Ta queue de paon fait les tables tournantes avec des pans de jungle (fanfares de sèves en marche) mais mon foie est plus acide et mes vénéfices plus forts que tes maléfices. Le lynch c'est six heures du soir dans la boue des bayous c'est un mouchoir noir agité au haut du mât d'un bateau pirate c'est le point de strangulation de l'ongle au carmin d'une interjection c'est la pampa c'est le ballet de la reine c'est la sagacité de la science c'est le coït inoubliable. O lynch sel mercure et antimoine! Le lynch est le sourire bleu d'un dragon ennemi des anges le lynch est une orchidée trop belle pour porter de fruits le lynch est une entrée en matière le lynch c'est la main du vent ensanglantant une forêt dont les arbres sont des galles qui brandissent dans leur main le flambeau vif de leur phallus châtré, le lynch est une main saupoudrée de poussière de pierres précieuses, le lynch est un lâcher de colibris, le lynch est un lapsus, le lynch est un coup de trompette un disque fêlé de gramophone une queue de cyclone à la traîne portée par des becs roses d'oiseaux rapaces. Le lynch est une belle chevelure que l'effroi rejette sur mon visage le lynch est un temple ruiné par les racines et sanglé de forêt vierge. O lynch aimable compagnon bel œil giclé large bouche muette hormis qu'un branle y répand le délire d'une morve tisse bien, éclair, sur ton métier un continent qui éclate en îles un oracle qui glisse en contorsion en scolopendre une lune qui installe sur la brèche le paon de soufre qui se lève dans la meurtrière sommaire de mon ouïe assassinée.

Lynch I

Why does spring grab me by the throat? what does it want of me? so what if it does not have enough spears and banners! I jeer at you spring for flaunting your blind eye and your bad breath. Your debauchery your corrupt kisses. Your peacock's tail makes spirit tables turn with patches of jungle (fanfares of marching sap) but my liver is more acidic and my venefice stronger than your malefice. Lynch it's 6 P.M. in the mud of the bayou it's a black handkerchief fluttering atop a pirate ship mast it's the strangulation point of a fingernail in the carmine of an interjection it's the pampa it's the queen's ballet it's the sagacity of science it's the unforgettable coitus. O lynch salt mercury and antimony! Lynch is the blue smile of a dragon enemy of angels lynch is an orchid too lovely to bear fruit lynch is an entry into matter lynch is the hand of the wind bloodying a forest whose trees are galls brandishing in their hands the living flame of their castrated phalli, lynch is a hand sprinkled with the dust of precious stones, lynch is a release of hummingbirds, lynch is a lapse, lynch is a trumpet blast a broken gramophone record a cyclone's tail dragged by the pink beaks of raptors. Lynch is a gorgeous chevelure that dread flings into my face lynch is a temple destroyed by roots and gripped by a virgin forest. O lynch loveable companion beautiful squirted eye huge mouth mute unless a jerking there spills the delirium of mucus weave well, lightning bolt, on your loom a continent exploding into islands an oracle contortedly slithering like a scolopendra a moon settling in the breech the sulfur peacock ascending in the succinct murderess-hole of my assassinated hearing.

Dévoreur

Le bouclier des mollusques
les mandibules des fourmis
les grands jeux du mimétisme à jeter bas le masque des phasmes et des pharaons
la dialectique du cuivre
l'aldébaran matutinal
se peut-il que fasse
                face de vie ou de mort
                une feuille mal jouée publiée par le vent
va caret couché sur le dos par la main perfide du sable
claste iconoclaste tonnerre de non sans noms
bélier et beffroi
date choisie pour toutes les grandes offensives de printemps
coureur
avant-coureur
j'ai mangé ma proie
et mes yeux ont poussé comme des ignames d'un champ inédit
mes yeux sont plus durs que la pierre
mes yeux ont mis en croix ont lapidé ont flagellé ma cervelle
                ma cervelle
                      va et vient
                              en blouse blanche de logarithmes
et puisque nous parlons d'économie de pensée
tiens dévoreur
l'espace et le temps aimables serpents pince contre pince font une fornication trop belle pour l'épuisement de leur vésicule à venin enfantant à la face volubile de silence et d'écho un frai munificent d'ombilics et de champignons la distribution de la chaleur s'intensifie à des proportions collectives le long de la barre que je chauffe et féconde du suc hagard de mon haleine

Devourer

The buckler of mollusks
the mandibles of ants
the great games of mimicry for unmasking phasmids and pharaoh ants
the dialectic of copper
matutinal aldebaran
can it be that
              life and death face off
              a leaf badly played disseminated by the wind
goes hawksbill overturned by the sand's perfidious hand
clast iconoclast thunder of nameless no
battering ram and belfry
the date chosen for all great spring offensives
cursor
precursor
I've eaten my prey
and my eyes have grown like yams in an original field
my eyes are harder than stone
my eyes have crucified have lapidated have flagellated my brain
         my brain
                 comes and goes
                           in the white blouse of logarithms
and since we are talking about the economy of thought
hold on devourer
space and time loveable serpents pincer to pincer create a fornication too
beautiful for the exhaustion of their venom vesicle giving birth in the voluble
face of silence and of echo to a munificent spawn of umbilici and mushrooms
the distribution of heat intensifies in collective proportions along the bar that
I heat and fecundate with the haggard sap of my breath

La loi est nue

Baies ailées j'ai marché sur le cœur grondant de l'excellent printemps
de qui ai-je jamais soutiré autre femme
qu'un long cri et sous ma traction de lait
qu'une terre s'enfuyant blessée et reptile entre les dents de la forêt

net trop plein du jet
me voici
dans les arrières des eaux
et roucoulant vos scrupuleuses colombes
                    assis mets vrai pour les oiseaux

que toutes les trames en vain se nouent
que tous les moulins à prière à gauche tournent
que tous les fleuves lancent à la face des villes le gant souple et chaud d'un
paquet de mules noires et de tresses

Mais paix cris de femelle. Si douce on la croirait un crépi inventé pour
la fouille attentatoire de mes doigts. Paix. Vous tous fermez la porte aux
dromadaires. Il n'y a plus de machine à traire le matin qui n'est pas encore
monté. J'ai des mains bleues qui tout arrêtent. Ma langue est bleue. Bleus
mon or et l'orgueil du sang des maudits qui tournent vers moi la tête. Si vous
saviez. J'ai renversé toutes les pierres toutes les peines toutes les prières. Vite!
météore aux ailes de comète. Météore au cœur d'améthyste donne-moi le mot
de passe
météore au cœur de pélican friable
météore qui revient tous les dix ans sur les lieux du crime
météore pèlerin de Sibérie
tous mes cailloux sont d'offense
Point d'huile.
La loi est nue.

The Law Is Naked

Bays winged I walked on the rumbling heart of the excellent spring
from whom have I ever conned a woman
other than a long cry and under my tug of milk
other than an earth fleeing wounded and reptile between the forest's teeth

clear overflowing from the gush
here I am
in the backwaters
and cooing your scrupulous doves
· seated a real dish for the birds

let all the woofs in vain be knotted
let all the prayer wheels turn to the left
let all the rivers hurl into the cities' faces the hot and supple glove of a bundle
of black mules and tresses

But hush female cries. So soft one might think it a roughcast invented for my fingers' damaging excavation. Hush. All of you close the door against the dromedaries. There are no more milking machines for the morning that has yet to rise. I have blue hands that stop everything. My tongue is blue. Blue my gold and the arrogance of the blood of the damned who turn their heads toward me. If you knew. I have overturned all the stones all the pains all the prayers. Quickly! meteor in the comet's wings. Meteor in the amethyst's heart give me the password
meteor in the heart of the friable pelican
meteor returning every ten years to the scene of the crime
meteor Siberian pilgrim
all my pebbles are made of offense
No oil at all.
The law is naked.

La pluie

Après que j'eus par le fer par le feu par la cendre visité les lieux les plus célèbres de l'histoire après que j'eus par la cendre le feu la terre et les astres courtisé de mes ongles de chien sauvage et de ventouse le champ autoritaire des protoplasmes
Je me trouvai comme à l'accoutumée du temps jadis au milieu d'une usine de nœuds de vipère dans un gange de cactus dans une élaboration de pèlerinages d'épines—et comme à l'accoutumée j'étais salivé de membres et de langues nés mille ans avant la terre—et comme à l'accoutumée je fis ma prière matinale celle qui me préserve du mauvais œil et que j'adresse à la pluie sous la couleur aztèque de son nom

Pluie qui si gentiment laves l'académique vagin de la terre d'une injection perverse
Pluie toute puissante qui fais sauter le doigt des roches sur le billot
Pluie qui gaves une armée de vers comme n'en saurait nourrir une forêt de mûriers
Pluie stratège génial qui pousses sur la glace de l'air ton armée de zigzags de berges innombrables qui ne peut pas ne pas surprendre l'ennui le mieux gardé
Pluie ruche de guêpes beau lait dont nous sommes les porcelets
Pluie je vois tes cheveux qui sont une explosion continue d'un feu d'artifice de hura-crépitans
tes cheveux de fausses nouvelles aussitôt démenties
Pluie qui dans tes plus répréhensibles débordements n'as garde d'oublier que les jeunes filles du Chiriqui tirent soudain de leur corsage de nuit une lampe faite de lucioles émouvantes
Pluie inflexible qui ponds des œufs dont les larves sont si fières que rien ne peut les obliger à passer à la poupe du soleil et de le saluer comme un amiral
Pluie qui es l'éventail de poisson frais derrière lequel se cachent les races courtoises pour voir passer la victoire aux pieds sales
Salut à toi pluie reine au fond de l'éternel déesse dont les mains sont multiples et dont le destin est unique toi sperme toi cervelle toi fluide
Pluie capable de tout sauf de laver le sang qui coule sur les doigts des assassins des peuples surpris sous les hautes futaies de l'innocence

Rain

After I had by iron by fire by ash visited the most celebrated places in history after I had by ash fire earth and stars courted with my wild dog and leechlike fingernails the authoritarian field of protoplasms
I found myself as usual in the old days in the middle of a factory of vipers' nests in a ganges of cacti in an elaboration of thorny pilgrimages—and as usual I was salivated by limbs and tongues born a thousand years before the earth—and as usual I made my morning prayer the one that protects me from the evil eye and that I address to the rain under the aztec color of its name

Rain who so gently washes a perverse injection from the earth's academic vagina
All-powerful rain who on the chopping block makes the fingers of the rocks leap
Rain who force-feeds an army of worms no mulberry forest could nourish
Rain inspired strategist who pushes across the mirror of the air your zigzag army of numberless riverbanks that cannot not surprise the best-kept boredom
Rain wasp nest beautiful milk whose piglets we are
Rain I see your hair which is a perpetual explosion of sandbox tree fireworks your hair of misinformation promptly denied
Rain who in your most reprehensible excesses takes care not to forget that Chiriqui maidens pull suddenly from their night corsage a lamp of thrilling fireflies
Inflexible rain who lays eggs whose larvae are so proud that nothing can make them mount the stern of the sun and salute it like an admiral
Rain who is a fresh fish fan behind which courteous races hide to watch victory with its dirty feet pass by
Greetings to you queen rain in the depths of the eternal goddess whose hands are multiple and whose destiny is unique thou sperm thou brain thou fluid
Rain capable of everything except washing away the blood that flows on the fingers of the murderers of entire peoples surprised in the soaring forests of innocence

Allure

O montagne ô dolomies cœur d'oiseau sous mes mains d'enfant
ô icebergs ô revenants vieux dieux scellés en pleine gloire
et quand même autour du feu à trois pierres couronné d'un cercle vibrant
de tipules
un étang pour les noyés se renouvelle
province des morts vous heurtez en vain la rotation des routes où le spectacle
passe du palier de flammes vertes à la tranche de maléfices
allure combats avec moi je porte la tiare solaire
boue vieille sorcière fais des ronds
gong décuple la prison dont les combats d'animaux expérimentent la voix
des hommes conservés dans la pétrification des forêts de mille ans

ma chère penchons sur les filons géologiques

Velocity

O mountain oh dolomites bird heart under my childlike hands
oh icebergs oh ghosts old gods sealed in full glory
and even if around a three stone fire crowned with a quivering circle of tipulas
a pond for the drowned renews itself
province of the dead in vain you strike the rotation of roads where the
spectacle passes from the level of green flames to the edge of malefice
velocity fight with me I wear the solar tiara
mud old witch draw circles
gong multiply the prison whose animal fights experience the voices of men
preserved in the petrifaction of millennial forests

my dear let's lean on geological veins

Désastre

Tout insecte compté (le métal de l'herbe a cravaté leur gorge)
menstrue de cendre (remords de mandragore)
bond lent d'un chiffon tendant sa surprise de pains dont l'équipage pris
au piège dessèche tout litige
désastre
blocs
au bout de l'œil la gueule sous le bâillon de nuages
volcan écartelé géant de mystagogue le Bédouin de ce désert
devanture d'un tout doux de caraïbe roulant sur des os et des ans sa caravane
écoutée d'engloutis
pieds ou éclat quel quarteron de nègres ou de peaux rouges massacrés à la fin
de la nuit rengaine ta dégaine jamais née
et tes pieds portés par les eaux
      les restitue au tablier sans cris d'un strom présomptueux

Disaster

Every insect counted (the metal of the grass has seized their throats)
ashy menses (mandragora remorse)
slow leap of a rag handing out its surprise of loaves whose crew entrapped
dries out all litigation
disaster
blocks
at the eye's limit its mug gagged by clouds
quartered volcano mystagogical giant the Bedouin of this desert
display of an oh so docile Carib rolling over bones and years his caravan
heard by ensurfed
feet or eruption what quadroon of niggers or redskins massacred at the end
of the night resheathes the dagger of your neverborn swagger
restituting your feet borne along by the waters
       to the screamless apron of a presumptuous strom

Société secrète

Du lagon monte une odeur de sang et une armée de mouches qui colportent
aux femmes la fraude des bijoux de la ménopause
l'état-major du crime s'est installé très confortablement sur le passage
de l'histoire dont l'épilepsie n'a jamais été si grande que dans ce temps
où chaque inscription est une aventure dont chaque lettre saute en paquets
de cartouches
une affinité de poussière conduit aux semaines qui sont les rainures
coulissières d'une guillotine devant laquelle l'accusateur public monte
la garde
en tout état de cause l'élévation et la chute du corps avertissent à tout
moment de l'étape atteinte par la digestion toujours difficile des avatars
géologiques
on n'a que faire des taupes qui gonflaient la terre de la poussée saisonnière
de l'insurrection
on n'a que faire du soleil c'est une fille violée qui n'ose plus rentrer à la
maison en tient lieu une contre-pluie de sable et de boue dont l'offensive
au-dessus des villes imite la perfection d'indiscipline des troupes de la
lumière polarisée
au demeurant
en dépit des antilopes amygdales qui se réunissent après une longue course
à l'aube de palmiers que font les pleurs sous les cous aimés et que ne
chassera jamais la main sagace des consolations

(pas plus qu'une superstition n'entamera le bel arbre réservé à la hache des
cœurs idolâtres en dépit du sang qui peint les billots et jette au travers de son
masque le bouquet de fleurs prématuré d'un scalp)

bise
et couteaux des astres
échangeons avec les satellites convexes
le petit salut aidant
que nous échangeons avec l'ortolan des neiges ensoleillé pour nous seuls à la
décriée des fragiles lucarnes d'où le contre-poison lance à l'ordinaire de son
ciel peu loquace
le train des sauveteurs de la mer
sur les rails de ce val dépêché à mon gré
au fond de la caillasse muletière d'une catastrophe sans repères

Secret Society

From the lagoon rises an odor of blood and an army of flies peddling to
women the fraud of menopausal jewels
the crime staff has settled very comfortably into the passing of history
whose epilepsy has never been so great as now when each inscription is an
adventure each letter of which explodes in packets of cartridges
a dusty affinity leads to weeks that are the outside railings of a guillotine
before which the public accuser stands guard
in any case the body's elevation and fall constantly warn of the stage reached
by the ever difficult digestion of geologic avatars
we have nothing to do with the moles that bulged up the earth with
insurrection's seasonal thrust
we have nothing to do with the sun it's a raped girl who no longer dares to
return home in its place a counter-rain of sand and mud whose offensive
above the cities imitates the undisciplined perfection of the troops of
polarized light
be that as it may
despite the tonsillar antelopes who merge after a long race in the palm-tree
dawn formed by tears beneath the beloved necks and which the sagacious
hand of constellations shall never chase away

(no more than a superstition shall broach the beautiful tree reserved for the
axe of idolatrous hearts despite the blood that paints the executioner blocks
and flings through its mask flower bouquets premature by a scalp)

north wind
and knives of the stars
let us exchange with convex satellites
the helpful little salute
that we exchange with the snow bunting solarized for us alone to the decry
of fragile skylights from which the counter-poison with its barely loquacious
heaven ordinarily casts
the train of sea rescuers
onto the tracks of this vale dispatched as I please
at the bottom of the mule marl of an unmarked catastrophe

Traversée nocturne

Audace c'est ce qui nous consolera le moins
voici l'alliage animal du muscle et de la voix dans la détonation pluvieuse
de la journée
sous le signe   *plus*   survolé d'une escadre de pétrels
Merci aux fermiers qui me régalent d'une haine peinte sur leur visage
les jours ne se perchent que sur l'épaule des femmes mieux qu'endormies
Orage ou pluie
à bonne fin les conduiront
les becs qui m'ont remis entre les mains du cri

Couvert d'encéphale frais
je m'élève déjà bien plus vite
        silence
                comme sous la masse le taureau
                c'est un baiser puisant des lèvres
                dans l'empreinte de nos sabots

Nocturnal Crossing

Audacity that is what shall console us least
right here is the animal alloy of muscle and voice in the rainy detonation
of the day
under the   *plus*   sign overflown by a squadron of petrels
Thanks to the farmers who regale me with hatred painted on their faces
days perch solely on the shoulders of women more than asleep
Storm or rain
the beaks that put me back between the hands of the scream
shall guide them laudably

Covered with fresh encephalon
I rise already even faster
       silence
              like the bull under the maul
              it is a kiss deriving lips
              from our clogprints

Entre autres massacres

De toutes leurs forces le soleil et la lune s'entrechoquent
les étoiles tombent comme des témoins trop mûrs
et comme une portée de souris grises

ne crains rien apprête tes grosses eaux
qui si bien emportent la berge des miroirs

ils ont mis de la boue sur mes yeux
et vois je vois terriblement je vois
de toutes les montagnes de toutes les îles
il ne reste plus rien que les quelques mauvais chicots
de l'impénitente salive de la mer

Among Other Massacres

With all their strength the sun and the moon collide
the stars fall like overripe warning lights
like a litter of gray mice

fear nothing prepare your high waters
that sweep away the bank of mirrors

they have put mud over my eyes
and I see I see terribly I see
of all the mountains of all the islands
nothing is left save the few rotted tooth stumps
of the impenitent saliva of the sea

Le griffon

Je suis un souvenir qui n'atteint pas le seuil
et erre dans les limbes où le reflet d'absinthe
quand le cœur de la nuit souffle par ses évents
bouge l'étoile tombée où nous nous contemplons

Le ciel lingual a pris sa neuve consistance de crème de noix fraîche ouverte
du coco

Andes crachant et Mayumbé sacré
seul naufrage que l'œil bon voilier nous soudoie
quand âme folle déchiquetée folle
      par les nuages qui m'arrivent dans les poissons bien clos
je remonte hanter la sinistre épaisseur des choses

The Griffin

I am a memory that does not reach the threshold
and wanders in limbo where the glint of absinthe
when the heart of night breathes through its blowholes
moves the fallen star in which we contemplate ourselves

The lingual sky took on a new consistency of a freshly opened coconut's cream

Spitting Andes and sacred Mayumbé
sole shipwreck that the eye good sailer pays off for us
when soul mad shredded mad
        through clouds that reach me in tightly shut fish
I reascend to haunt the sinister thickness of things

Rachat

Le bruit fort gravite pourri d'une cargaison
désastre véreux et clair de soldanelle
le bruit fort gravite méninge de diamants
ton visage glisse nu en ma fureur laiteuse

Touffeurs d'amibes
touffeurs de laitances vrais fils de la vraie vierge immaculée aux aubes de la
mer quand les méteils firent peau et maraudes de damnés

Touffeurs de tas d'assiettes ébréchées
de ruines de chiens pelés et de scaphandriers qui glissent au crépuscule

Touffeur fruste rayonnement
au nu très lent de ma main
l'ombilic vierge de la terre

Redemption

The loud noise gravitates rotten with cargo
wormy and bright disaster of a soldanella
the loud noise gravitates meninx of diamonds
your face glides naked into my milky frenzy

Amoebic swelter
miltic swelter true gossamers of the true immaculate virgin in the auroras
of the sea when the maslin made skin and plunder of the damned

Sweltering pile of chipped plates
of ruins of hairless dogs and of deep-sea divers who glide away at dusk

Swelter crude radiance
in the very slow nakedness of my hand
virgin umbilicus of the earth

Mississipi

Hommes tant pis qui ne vous apercevez pas que mes yeux se souviennent
    de frondes et de drapeaux noirs
        qui assassinent à chaque battement de mes cils de Mississipi

Hommes tant pis qui ne voyez pas qui ne voyez rien
pas même la très belle signalisation de chemin de fer que font sous mes
paupières les disques rouges et noirs du serpent-corail que ma munificence
love dans mes larmes de Mississipi

Hommes tant pis qui ne voyez pas qu'au fond du réticule où le hasard a
déposé nos yeux de Mississipi
il y a qui attend un buffle noyé jusqu'à la garde des yeux du marécage

Hommes tant pis qui ne voyez pas que vous ne pouvez m'empêcher de bâtir
à sa suffisance
des îles à la tête d'œuf de ciel flagrant
sous la férocité calme du géranium immense de notre soleil.

Mississipi

Too bad for you men who don't notice that my eyes remember
        slings and black flags
           that murder with each blink of my Mississipi lashes

Too bad for you men who do not see who do not see anything
not even the gorgeous railway signals formed under my eyelids by the
black and red discs of the coral snake that my munificence coils in my
Mississipi tears

Too bad for you men who do not see that in the depth of the reticule where
chance has deposited our Mississipi eyes
there waits a buffalo sunk to the very hilt of the swamp's eyes

Too bad for you men who do not see that you cannot stop me from building
to his fill
egg-headed islands of flagrant sky
under the calm ferocity of the immense geranium of our sun.

Blues

Aguacero
beau musicien
au pied d'un arbre dévêtu
parmi les harmonies perdues
près de nos mémoires défaites
parmi nos mains de défaite
et des peuples de force étrange
nous laissions pendre nos yeux
et natale
dénouant la longe d'une douleur
nous pleurions.

Blues

Aguacero
beautiful musician
unclothed at the foot of a tree
amidst the lost harmonies
close to our defeated memories
amidst our hands of defeat
and peoples of a strength strange
we let our eyes hang
and native
loosing the leading-rein of a sorrow
we wept.

Le bouc émissaire

Les veines de la berge s'engourdissent d'étranges larves
nous et nos frères
dans les champs les squelettes attendent leurs frissons et la chair rien ne
        viendra et la saison est nulle
la morsure de nos promesses s'est accomplie au-dessus du sein d'un village
        et le village est mort avec tous ses hommes qu'on ne reconnaissait
        à travers leur tube de mica hier qu'à la patience violette de leurs
        excréments muets
O cueilleuse crépusculaire
si fragile si fragile au bord des nuits la pâtisserie du paysage qu'à la fin
        jubilation à tête blanche des pygargues elle y vole mais pour l'œil
        qui se voit il y a sur la paroi prophète d'ombre et tremblant au gré
        des pyrites un cœur qui pompe un sang de lumière et d'herbe
et la mer l'Arborigène une poignée de rumeurs entre les dents se traîne
        hors de ses os marsupiaux et posant sa première pierre d'île dans le
        vent qui s'éboule de la force renouvelée des fœtus, rumine flamber
        ses punchs d'anathèmes et de mirage vers la merveille nue de nos
        villes tâtant le futur et nos gueules claquantes de bouc émissaire

The Scapegoat

The veins of the river bank grow numb with strange larvae
us and our brothers
in the fields the skeletons await their tremors and their flesh nothing shall
    come and the season is null
the bite of our promises was fulfilled above the breast of a village and the
    village died with all its men recognizable through their mica tubes
    yesterday only by the violet patience of their mute excrement
O crepuscular gatherer
so fragile so fragile at the edge of the nights the pastry of the landscape that
    at last a white-headed jubilation of sea eagles she flies there but for
    the eye that sees itself there is on the wall prophet of shadows and
    trembling at the whim of pyrites a heart pumping a blood made of
    light and grass
and the sea the Arboriginal a handful of murmurs between its teeth drags
    itself out of its marsupial bones and placing its first island rock in
    the wind which tumbles down from the renewed strength of fetuses,
    ponders igniting its punch of anathemas and mirage against the
    naked wonder of our cities probing the future and our chattering
    scapegoat mugs

Transmutation

Un arbre pousse contre un mur sa querelle de tuyau tordu
en l'absence de toute référence objective les cataractes ont suspendu aux
fenêtres le linge que les femmes hygiéniques tachent de leurs menstrues si
bien que rien n'est plus individuel que le saccage du temps
seul le cou tanné des prostituées donne encore le sens de l'infini
J'ai beau expliquer que je n'ai pas démérité on me laisse seul
défense c'est ce que me hurle incessamment un orage
toujours annoncé toujours différé qui alimente l'inconscient de nos foules
de toutes les péripéties du cauchemar
Heureusement on ne s'est point aperçu que je me suis aperçu que j'ai
des mains pour me tenir compagnie j'ai mes mains de queue de singe j'ai
des mains d'attrape-nigaud j'ai mes mains d'assassin j'ai mes mains de
somnambule et parfois quand bat à mon pouls le laps du remords monté
de l'Atlantide j'ai mes mains de coquillage j'ai aussi mes mains de guano
qui sont si belles qu'on les appelle des sierras Nevadas j'ai mes mains de
pigeon-vole j'ai mes mains de scaphandre j'ai aussi mes mains à bercer les
petits enfants qui viennent à moi car mon exercice le plus spirituel consiste
à essayer de m'arrêter moi-même j'ai des mains de juste qui sous l'effet du
mildiou n'arrivent jamais à maturation mes mains incendiaires mes mains
bicolores mes mains à fièvre miliaire mes mains généralement quelconques
mes mains de plongeurs de perles qui ont l'habitude des profondeurs
Pour les jours de pluie j'ai mes curieuses mains d'otaries que je ne décrirai
pas car ce serait un sacrilège
Les jours de fête j'ai ces mains somptueuses que l'empereur ancien revêtait
à Cuzco pour accueillir le soleil j'ai mes mains qui sont des miroirs à mettre
le feu à mes mains à servir d'épouvantail aux oiseaux du solstice

Transmutation

A tree thrusts against a wall its quarrel of twisted pipe
in the absence of any objective reference the cataracts have hung in their
windows the laundry that hygienic women soil with their menses to such
an extent that nothing is more personal than the sacking of time
the tanned necks of prostitutes alone still give meaning to the infinite
However much I point out that I have not proved unworthy they leave
me alone
defense a storm screams at me incessantly
always foretold always deferred nourishing the unconscious of our crowds
with all the peripeteia of nightmare
Happily they did not notice that I noticed that I have my hands to keep me
company I have my monkey tail hands I have my booby-trap hands I have my
assassin hands I have my sleepwalker hands and sometimes when my pulse
beats the lapse of remorse risen from Atlantis I have my shell hands I also
have my guano hands that are so lovely they are called Sierra Nevadas I have
my "pigeon flies" hands I have my diving-suit hands I also have my hands for
rocking the little children who come to me since my most spiritual exercise
consists in trying to stop myself I have righteous hands which affected by
mildew never become mature my incendiary hands my bicolored hands my
miliary fever hands my generally insignificant hands my pearl-diver hands
that are accustomed to the depths
For rainy days I have my curious, eared seal hands that I shall not describe
for that would be a sacrilege
On feast days I have these sumptuous hands that the old emperor donned
in Cuzco to greet the sun I have my hands that are mirrors for setting fire
to my hands to serve as a scarecrow for the birds of the solstice

Demeure I

Je t'emmerde geôlier
la fièvre avec aux dents le poignard des razzias la fièvre avec aux dents
la parole des torrents
la fièvre cheval de race doux faucon
de son palanquin me précède
Demeure faite de défaites
demeure faite de carènes vives
demeure faite de passiflore
demeure cent fois faite et défaite
demeure faite de dents de requins
ah sacrée demeure faite de tonnerres de dieu et de l'éclair
des sombres sucs qui sommeillent dans mes grands ceibas
le cri qui maudit n'existe plus sur moi
le mal de chaîne qui arrête nos chevilles
le mal de carcan qui pèse sur nos épaules
tout cela est dissipé dépouillé comme cet épi
dissipé comme l'anse accroche la lumière du beau temps au bol de bruit
de la mer
dépouillé comme toi Volcan qui du sommet de ton crime te précipites
dans le suicide pour rejoindre au fond de la mer tes complices à naître
méditatifs marsouins et qui attendent

Dwelling I

Screw you jailer
fever with its razzia dagger in its teeth fever with its torrential word in
its teeth
fever thoroughbred horse sweet falcon
with its palanquin preceding me
Dwelling made of defeats
dwelling made of living ships' hulls
dwelling made of passionflower
dwelling made and remade a hundred times
dwelling made of sharks' teeth
ah hallowed dwelling made of flashing hell and damnation
of somber saps dozing in my massive ceibas
the screaming curse upon me no longer exists
the chain evil that checks our ankles
the iron collar evil that presses heavily on our shoulders
all that has been dissipated stripped away like this kernel
dissipated like the bay catching the light of fine weather in the noise bowl
of the sea
stripped bare like you Volcano who at the peak of your crime hurl yourself
into suicide to rejoin in the sea's depths your accomplices the pensive
porpoises yet to be born and who wait

Le coup de couteau du soleil dans le dos des villes surprises

Et je vis un premier animal
il avait un corps de crocodile des pattes d'équidé une tête de chien mais
lorsque je regardai de plus près à la place des bubons c'étaient des cicatrices
laissées en des temps différents par les orages sur un corps longtemps
soumis à d'obscures épreuves
sa tête je l'ai dit était des chiens pelés que l'on voit rôder autour des
volcans dans les villes que les hommes n'ont pas osé rebâtir et que hantent
éternellement les âmes des trépassés
et je vis un second animal
il était couché sous un bois de dragonnier des deux côtés de son museau de
chevrotain comme des moustaches se détachaient deux rostres enflammés
aux pulpes
Je vis un troisième animal qui était un ver de terre mais un vouloir étrange
animait la bête d'une longue étroitesse et il s'étirait sur le sol perdant et
repoussant sans cesse des anneaux qu'on ne lui aurait jamais cru la force
de porter et qui se poussaient entre eux la vie très vite comme un mot de
passe très obscène

Alors ma parole se déploya dans une clairière de paupières sommaires,
velours sur lequel les étoiles les plus filantes allaient leurs ânesses

le bariolage sauta livré par les veines d'une géante nocturne
ô la maison bâtie sur roc la femme glaçon du lit la catastrophe perdue comme
une aiguille dans une botte de foin
une pluie d'onyx tomba et de sceaux brisés sur un monticule dont aucun
prêtre d'aucune religion n'a jamais cité le nom et dont l'effet ne peut se
comparer qu'aux coups de fouet d'une étoile sur la croupe d'une planète
sur la gauche délaissant les étoiles disposer le vever de leurs nombres les
nuages ancrer dans nulle mer leurs récifs le cœur noir blotti dans le cœur
de l'orage
nous fondîmes sur demain avec dans nos poches le coup de couteau très
violent du soleil dans le dos des villes surprises

The Sun's Knife-Stab in the Back of the Surprised Cities

And I saw a first animal
it had a crocodile body equine feet a dog's head but when I looked more
closely in place of buboes were scars left at different times by storms on
a body long subjected to obscure trials
its head I told you was that of the hairless dogs one sees prowling around
the volcanoes in cities that men have not dared to rebuild and that the souls
of the dead haunt for all eternity
and I saw a second animal
it was lying beneath a dragon tree from both sides of its musk-deer muzzle
two pulp-enflamed rostra stood out like mustaches
I saw a third animal that was an earthworm but a strange will animated the
beast with a long narrowness and it stretched out on the ground ceaselessly
losing and growing new rings that one would never have thought it strong
enough to bear and that pushed life back and forth among them very fast
like an obscene password

Then my word unfolded in a glade of pithy, velvet eyelids over which the
fastest falling stars breast-fed their she-asses

the motley array exploded surrendered by the veins of a nocturnal giantess
oh the house built upon rock the woman ice cube of the bed the catastrophe
lost like a needle in a bundle of hay
a rain of onyx and of broken seals fell upon a hillock whose name has never
been uttered by any priest of any religion and whose effect can only be
compared to a star's whiplashes on a planet's rump
on the left deserting the stars to arrange the *vever* of their numbers the
clouds to anchor in no sea their reefs the black heart crouched in the heart
of the storm
we built on tomorrow having pocketed the sun's very violent knife-stab in
the back of the surprised cities

À l'heure où dans la chaleur les moines nus descendent de l'Himalaya

Très fort pendant les moustiques montés des volutes chargées à mitraille des maremmes joli cœur de la brutalité à la patte moricaude des bouges de sangliers

Très fort pendant les grands fleuves qui à la vermine débranchent leurs cuisses très immondes lèvres bleues giclant un rire cru de vagin

Très fort pendant la face molle des pollens s'écrasant dans la conspiration du vent et les cheminées qui fument sous le tunnel des épaules des fauves en escarboucles d'yeux plus tendres que leur alentour de graminées

Très fort monstre contre monstre
le tien dont le corps est une statue de suc de bois rouge
dont le crachat est un pissat de fofa
le mien dont la sueur est un jet de bile de caïman

que je les sorte enfin comme une nuit pluvieuse de cris d'alouates de ma poitrine si tendre de fausse oronge

When in the Heat of the Day Naked Monks Descend the Himalayas

Very powerful pendant the mosquitoes equipped with maremma grapeshot-loaded volutes gigolo of brutality with wild boar wallow darky feet

Very powerful pendant the great rivers that verminously disconnect their really filthy thighs blue lips spurting a raw vaginal laugh

Very powerful pendant the soft face of pollen getting ground up in the wind's conspiracy and the smoking chimneys under the tunnel of the shoulders of carbuncular wild beasts with eyes tenderer than their grassy surroundings

Very powerful monster against monster
yours whose body is a statue of red woody sap
whose spittle is fofa urine
mine whose sweat is a gush of caiman bile

let me dislodge them finally like a night rainy with howler monkey cries
from my chest as tender as fly agaric

Attentat aux mœurs

Nuit dure nuit gaule sans étoile. Je suis très mal avec l'espace. Qu'importe. Nuit sale haillon arbre fou je suis très mal avec le Temps. Qu'importe? Plus loin que le miroir plus loin que toute la vie revue dans l'accident où elle afflue très vite plus loin que les cités oubliées plus loin que les rites au sens désappris plus loin même que l'autruche qui emporte les lettres que je feins de ne pas écrire plus loin que mon petit cheval que je cache jalousement parce qu'il s'est enfui de toutes les races plus loin que les pièces d'or que répand la cervelle du soleil dans la pensée du taudis plus loin que les hauts gants blancs que les sommets revêtent pour accueillir le vent
ton regard plonge-le, Monstre, dans le bien-fondé d'un abîme alimenté à un vivier de monstres
Je suis très mal avec l'espace très mal avec le temps. Qu'importe. À travers le voyage que fréquente une haute fumigation de coups de fouet sur un pavé fait de petits naufrages à la traverse des bourgs où les alérions végètent enchâssés comme des saints dans les belles postures du paludisme
trébuchant—à la ceinture un cliquetis de clés qui de portes n'ouvrent que celle du couloir aux pythons la même au demeurant qui donne sur le mauvais temps qui de l'Atlantique toujours vient—un mendiant sonne dans la rue qui comme avec indifférence encercle de sel gemme l'énergie massive des ténèbres
cependant que les masses compactes des icebergs pirates tendent vers Ostende

Attack on Morals

Hard night long pole night without stars. I am on very bad terms with space.
So what. Dirty night crazed tree rag I am on very bad terms with time. So
what? Farther than the mirror farther than all life reviewed in the accident
where it surges very rapidly farther than forgotten cities farther than rites
with forgotten meanings farther even than the ostrich that carries the letters
I pretend not to write farther than my little horse that I jealously hide because
it fled each and every race farther than the gold pieces that the sun's brain
scatters in the hovel's thought farther than the tall white gloves that summits
put on to greet the wind
your gaze plunge it, Monster, into the validity of an abyss fed by a fish tank
of monsters
I am on very bad terms with space very bad terms with time. So what. Across
the journey frequented by a lofty fumigation of whiplashes on a pavement
made of little shipwrecks thwarting towns where allerions vegetate enshrined
like saints in the noble postures of paludism
stumbling—at his belt a clicking of keys that by way of doors open only onto
the python corridor the same after all that opens to the bad weather inevitably
in from the Atlantic—a beggar tolls in the street which as if indifferently
encircles with rock salt the massive energy of darkness
while compact masses of pirate icebergs tack toward Ostende

Fils de la Foudre

Et sans qu'elle ait daigné séduire les geôliers
à son corsage s'est délité un bouquet d'oiseaux-mouches
à ses oreilles ont germé des bourgeons d'atolls
elle me parle une langue si douce que tout d'abord je ne comprends pas
mais à la longue je devine qu'elle m'affirme que le printemps est arrivé
à contre-courant
que toute soif est étanchée que l'automne nous est concilié
que les étoiles dans la rue ont fleuri en plein midi et très bas suspendent leurs fruits

Son of Thunder

And without her deigning to seduce the jailers
at her bosom a bouquet of hummingbirds has exfoliated
at her ears buds of atolls have sprouted
she speaks a language to me so sweet that at first I do not understand but
eventually I surmise she is assuring me that spring has come counter-current
that all thirst is quenched that autumn is kindly disposed to us
that the stars in the street have blossomed at high noon and dangle their
fruits very low

Laissez-passer

Facile prolongement de la déglutition par la trismégiste bouche obscène
d'un marais au ventre brun
gluants droseras d'une gadoue heureuse écoutant dans leurs lèvres quelle
nouvelle fraternelle leurs jours sont de rigueur sur ce monde noué de trop
de fumées d'haleines masquant la verve de poivre de l'orage

Penche penche sur l'abîme sur le vertige
penche penche sur le néant
penche penche sur l'incendie

mais même en plein ciel je retrouve mille couteaux effilés
mille clés de lassos mille curés de corbeaux

hurle frappe le rocher et la terre je la peuple de poissons
que surgissent sur les usines des drapeaux
et sonne ta cohorte sonne ton renouveau de flammes
sonne ton dais d'argent
sonne l'arroi et le désarroi
sonne tes cuillers de paratonnerre
sonne tes sabots d'onyx
sonne ton horizon d'araignée
sonne tes cassolettes
sonne tes petits verres tordus par le désastre
sonne tes gémissements
sonne tes éclats de grenade
Je supporte le long des méridiens la marche sourde des opulents pèlerins
que font les forêts mordues par la rage
ébranlement
Groenland
hyènes dédaigneuses qui me flairez je ne suis pas au désert! l'air s'arrête
j'entends le grincement des pôles autour de leurs essieux l'air bruit j'assiste
impuissant à l'ensauvagement de mon esprit l'air m'apporte le Zambèze
Les bambous semblent aux multiples arêtes le squelette d'un immense
poisson des âges géologiques planté en guise de totem par une peuplade
disparue.

Permit

Easy prolongation of deglutition by the obscene trismegistic mouth of a
brown-bellied marsh
sticky sundews of a happy muck listening in their lips what fraternal news
their days are *de rigueur* in this world knotted by too much smoky breath
masking the peppery verve of the storm

Lean lean on the abyss on vertigo
lean lean on nothingness
lean lean on conflagration

but even in midair I rediscover a thousand sharpened knives
a thousand keys to lassos a thousand priestly crows

howl strike the rock and the earth I people it with fish
let flags loom over the factories
and sound your cohort sound your renewal in flames
sound your silver dais
sound your array and disarray
sound your lightning-rod spoons
sound your onyx clogs
sound your arachnoid horizon
sound your cassolettes
sound your little glasses twisted by disaster
sound your groanings
sound your grenade shrapnel
I bear along the meridians the deaf procession of opulent pilgrims made up
of rabies-bitten forests
perturbation
Greenland
hyenas disdainfully sniff me I am not in the desert! the air pauses I hear
the grating of poles on their axles the air drones I impotently attend the
decivilization of my mind the air brings me the Zambezi
Bamboo stalks seem to be the multiple bones of an immense fish skeleton
planted in some geological age in the guise of a totem by an extinct
small tribe.

Solide

cré nom de Dieu ils ont assuré l'univers et tout pèse—tout—le fil à plomb de la gravité s'étant installé au fond facile de la solitude—les gisements d'uranium les statues des jardins les amours perverses la rue qui seulement feint d'être fluide la rivière n'en parlons pas dont les trains plus pesants que mes pieds il n'est pas jusqu'au soleil qui n'ait arrêté ses nuages à jamais fixes. Fixe c'est d'ailleurs le commandement qui sans cesse retentit d'un bout à l'autre sur tout le front de cette étrange armée du désespoir. Le monde se fixe. La pierre est fixe. L'immense faux mouvement est fixe et parle-moi de tes allures de petite folle que circonscrit le monde qui circonscrit un fleuve où chaque couple est sommé de se baigner deux fois et d'où d'ailleurs ne surgiront jamais les vraies vaches de la débâcle avec son ranch de crochets et de racines.
Je suis une pierre couverte de ruines. Je suis une île chaperonnée de guano. Je suis une pyramide plantée par une dynastie disparue de toute mémoire un troupeau d'éléphants une piqûre de moustiques une petite ville agrandie par le crime à moins que ce ne soit la guerre du Pacifique ou la charte de l'Atlantique. Il y a des gens qui prétendent qu'ils pourraient reconstituer un homme à partir de son sourire. C'est pourquoi je me garde de laisser mes empreintes dentales se mouler dans le mastic de l'air.
Visage de l'homme tu ne bougeras point
tu es pris dans les coordonnées féroces de mes rides.

Solid

holy shit they insured the universe and everything weighs—everything—
the plumb line of gravity having been installed at the facile bottom of
solidity—the uranium deposits the garden statues the perverse loves the
street that merely pretends to be fluid the stream don't mention it whose
trains heavier than my feet there is nothing up to and including the sun that
has not stopped its clouds forever fixed. Fixed is moreover the command
that ceaselessly resounds from one end to the other along the entire front of
this strange army of despair. The world is fixed. Stone is fixed. The immense
false movement is fixed and tell me about the ways of your little mad girl
circumscribed by the world that circumscribes a river where each couple is
summoned to bathe twice and from where moreover the true cows of the
debacle with its ranch of hooks and roots shall never rush forth.
I am a stone covered by ruins. I am an island falcon-hooded by guano.
I am a pyramid planted by a dynasty vanished from all memory a herd of
elephants a mosquito bite a small city aggrandized by crime unless it be the
war in the Pacific or the Atlantic Charter. There are those who claim they can
reconstruct a man from his smile. That's why I am careful not to let my dental
impression be molded in the putty of the air.
Face of man you shall not budge
you are caught in the ferocious coordinates of my wrinkles.

La femme et la flamme

Un morceau de lumière qui descend la source d'un regard
l'ombre jumelle du cil et de l'arc en ciel sur le visage
et alentour
qui va là angélique
et amble
Femme le temps qu'il fait
le temps qu'il fait peu m'importe
ma vie est toujours en avance d'un ouragan
tu es le matin qui fond sur le fanal une pierre de nuit entre les dents
tu es le passage aussi d'oiseaux marins
toi qui es le vent à travers les ipoméas salés de la connaissance
d'un autre monde s'insinuant
Femme
tu es un dragon dont la belle couleur s'éparpille et s'assombrit jusqu'à former
l'inévitable teneur des choses
j'ai coutume des feux de brousse
j'ai coutume des rats de brousse de la cendre et des ibis mordorés de la
flamme
Femme liant de misaine beau revenant
casque d'algues d'eucalyptus
                l'aube n'est-ce pas
                et au facile des lisses
                nageur très savoureux

The Woman and the Flame

A bit of light that descends the springhead of a gaze
twin shadow of the eyelash and the rainbow on a face
and round about
who goes there angelically
ambling
Woman the current weather
the current weather matters little to me
my life is always ahead of a hurricane
you are the morning that swoops down on the lamp a night stone between
its teeth
you are the passage of seabirds as well
you who are the wind through the salty ipomeas of consciousness
insinuating yourself from another world
Woman
you are a dragon whose lovely color is dispersed and darkens so as to
constitute the inevitable tenor of things
I am used to brush fires
I am used to ashen bush rats and the bronze ibis of the flame
Woman binder of the foresail gorgeous ghost
helmet of algae of eucalyptus
        dawn isn't it
        and in the abandon of the ribbands
        very savory swimmer

Millibars de l'orage

N'apaisons pas le jour et sortons la face nue
face aux pays inconnus qui coupent aux oiseaux leur sifflet
le guet-apens s'ouvre le long d'un bruit de confins de planètes.
ne fais pas attention aux chenilles qui tissent souple
une chair capable d'épaules et de seins
mais seulement aux millibars qui se plantent dans le mille d'on orage
à délivrer l'espace où se hérissent le cœur des choses et la venue de l'homme

Rêve n'apaisons pas
parmi les clous de chevaux fous
un bruit de larmes qui tâtonne vers l'aile immense des paupières

Millibars of the Storm

Let's not placate the day but go out face exposed
facing those unknown countries that cut off the birds' whistles
the ambush opens along a din of outer planetary borders.
pay no attention to the caterpillars supply weaving
a flesh capable of shoulders and breasts
but only to the millibars that position themselves in the bull's-eye of a storm
to liberate the space where bristles the heart of things and the advent of man

Dream let's not placate
amidst the nails of crazed horses
a noise of tears groping toward the eyelids' vast wing

Galanterie de l'histoire

Vierges d'Ogoué gratifiez-moi
d'une étoile dite nouvelle
d'un prêtre couché sur la mer en joue comme un tromblon
d'une chambre de torture de vingt pesetas avec dix *ave Maria*
pour que j'arrache toutes tes mauvaises pensées
pour que je débride tes plaies mauvaises mon petit ami
Séismes passez-moi la main
volcans donnez-moi du feu
bêtes du feu lancez-moi vos griffes
pour dévêtir les démons qui soufflent dans votre souffle mon grand ami pour
que je projette en miettes déjà de bombes
les eaux perverses qui me coulent sur la joue ma joue
celle de toi à moi à califourchon sur le sale toit du monde où de leurs pas
jaillit une voiture de pompiers très vite transformée par le sang en l'or dont
on fait les casques

et voilà défiant les pas qu'il y a dans Hyde Park et dans la succursale de la
Place de la République deux creuses cavités qui sont des yeux à redurcir
les nuages qui très attentivement regardent tel le spectacle d'un enfant
attendrissant l'impudique commencement de l'année goujate

et le sang qui de toute façon reflue très vite
d'un coup de pied d'un gabelou d'une chape de plomb d'un chapelet
de piastres d'une rizière décortiquée
apportant sur le plateau de la justice
des fromages de crachat le carat de l'insulte
et trois rois mages

Gallantry of History

Virgins of Ogou gratify me
with a star called new
with a priest lying on the sea taking aim with a blunderbuss
with a torture chamber of twenty pesetas with ten *ave Marias*
so that I can root out all your nasty thoughts
so that I can incise your nasty wounds my little friend
Give me a break earthquakes
give me a light volcanoes
flash me your claws glow-worms
to undress the demons that breathe in your breath my great friend so that I
project in bombs already smithereens
the perverse waters that flow down the cheek my cheek
that of yours to mine astraddle the dirty roof of the world where from their
steps surges a fire engine immediately transformed by blood into the gold
from which helmets are made

and so defying the steps there are in Hyde Park and in the annex of the Place
de la République two hollow cavities that are eyes for rehardening those
clouds gazing very attentively like the spectacle of a child tenderizing the
lewd beginning of a boorish year

and the blood that at all events ebbs very quickly
with a kick from a customs officer with a lead cope with a chaplet of piasters
with a hulled rice paddy
bearing on the salver of justice
spittle cheese the carat of an insult
and three wise men

À quelques milles de la surface

La pointe du cône d'ombre sur nos joues de Brésil
aux éclipses du soleil
si rieuse d'un bonheur comme le coït long
d'un arbre et d'un bateau à voiles
dans le hall d'un cyclone de première grandeur
Femme
donne-moi tes yeux d'aigle
tes yeux d'oiseau glorieux
tes yeux d'oiseau incendiaire et conducteur des âmes
et comme j'aime la circulation du sang du désastre
dans les veines d'une maison de dix étages à la minute sublime
qui précède son écroulement sur le coup de trois heures après midi

Several Miles from the Surface

The tip of the cone of shadow on our Brazilian cheeks
in the eclipses of the sun
laughing so with happiness like the long coitus
of a tree with a sailboat
in the hall of a cyclone of the first order
Woman
give me your eagle eyes
your glorious bird eyes
your incendiary bird and soul conductor eyes
and how I do love the circulation of the blood of disaster
in the veins of a ten-storied house at the sublime moment preceding
its collapse at the stroke of 3 P.M.

Chevelure

Dirait-on pas bombardé d'un sang de latérites
bel arbre nu
en déjà l'invincible départ vers on imagine un sabbat de splendeur et de villes
l'invincible et spacieux cri du coq

O cuve où surprendre le colloque du galop et du vent
O matière soleils de chiens girant dans le déclic de crochets de leur gel
innommable
O dans les savanes du silence les gloires sans visages se coulant dans
la creuse ténèbre des pistils

Innocente qui ondoies
tous les sucs qui montent dans la luxure de la terre
tous les poisons que distillent les alambics nocturnes dans l'involucre
des malvacées
tous les tonnerres des saponaires
sont pareils à ces mots discordants écrits par l'incendie des bûchers sur
les oriflammes sublimes de la révolte

Chevelure
flammes ingénues qui léchez un cœur insolite
peste tu planteras nos paysages dans la cassée vapeur d'un pré de phares et tu
feras signe à l'angoisse jouant avec des épaules attachées à des clapotis sans
jamais autour de la tête
le moindre halo d'un futur lu dans l'oubliette de l'attente
là où l'océan désigne au mépris des phrases matinales l'élaboration perfide
des diamants
innocente qui vas là je suis sous les futaies d'une chair qui me regarde
pour nous soyons attentifs et dociles
les visages endormis dans l'étouffement des schismes
sortiront à rendre inopérantes les inventions techniques les plus modernes
La forêt se souviendra de l'eau et de l'aubier
comme moi je me souviens du museau attendri
des grands fleuves qui titubent comme des aveugles
à la recherche de leurs yeux de purin
la forêt se souvient que le dernier mot ne peut être
que le cri flambant de l'oiseau des ruines dans le bol de l'orage
Innocent qui vas là

Chevelure

Wouldn't you have thought it bombarded by laterite blood
a beautiful stripped tree
the invincible and spacious cockcrow in the already invincible departure
toward an imagined witches' Sabbath of splendor and of cities

O vat in which to surprise the colloquium of the gallop and of the wind
O matter dog suns gyrating in the clicking hooks of their unnamable gel
O in the savannahs of silence the faceless glories flowing into the pistils' hollow gloom

Undulating innocent
all the juices rising in the lust of the earth
all the poisons that nocturnal alembics distill in the involucres of the malvaceae
all the saponarias' thunder
are like these discordant words written by the flaming of the pyres over the sublime oriflammes of your revolt

Chevelure
artless flames licking a rare heart
plague you shall fix our landscapes in the broken vapors of a meadow of lighthouses and you shall signal the anguish playing with shoulders attached to splashings but never around the head
the least halo of a future read in the oubliette of expectation
where the ocean designates a perfidious elaboration of diamonds to the scorn of matutinal phrases
innocent who ventures there I am under the forests of a flesh that watches me
that we be attentive and docile
sleeping faces in the stifling of schisms
shall emerge to render inoperable the most modern technical inventions
The forest shall remember the water and the sapwood
as I too remember the mollified snouts
of big rivers that stumble about like blind men
searching for their slurry eyes
the forest remembers that the last word can only be
the blazing cry of the bird of ruins in the bowl of the storm
Innocent who ventures there

oublie de te rappeler
que le baobab est notre arbre
qu'il mal agite ses bras si nains
qu'on le dirait un géant imbécile
et toi
séjour de mon insolence de mes tombes de mes trombes
crinière paquet de lianes espoir fort des naufragés
dors doucement au tronc méticuleux de mon étreinte ma femme
ma citadelle

forget to remember
that the baobab is our tree
that it badly waves arms so dwarfed
that one would take it for an imbecilic giant
and you
sojourn of my insolence of my tombs of my twisters
mane bundle of lianas stubborn hope of the shipwrecked
sleep softly in the meticulous trunk of my embrace my woman
my citadel

Scalp

Il est minuit
les sorciers ne sont pas encore venus
les montagnes n'ont pas fondu
ai-je assez dit à la terre
de ne pas s'installer par crainte de l'insolation ?
Me serrerai-je la gorge avec une corde faite du lierre de mes murmures ?
poissons cueilleuses de l'eau et son réceptacle
c'est par-dessus vos têtes que je parle
comme les étoiles dans la bave du miel de ses mauvais rêves et la terre elle
a enfanté sous nous

C'est vrai que j'ai laissé mes ongles en pleine chair de cyclone parmi le fracas
des hannetons gros
et jusqu'à faire jaillir le jaune neuf d'un sperme
me jetant sous son ventre pour mesurer
mon rut

Maintenant
par le sang dur du viol
entre deux criminels
je sais l'heure
celui qui meurt
celui qui s'en va
Mais un mais *moi*
enserré dans la touffe qui m'endort
et par la grâce des chiens
sous le vent innocent et déplisseur des lianes
héros de chasse casqué d'un oiseau d'or

Scalp

It is midnight
the sorcerers have not yet come
the mountains have not melted
have I sufficiently told the earth
not to set itself up for fear of sunstroke?
Shall I tighten my throat with a cord made from the ivy of my mutterings?
fish gatherers of water and its receptacle
it is above your heads that I speak
like the stars in the honey drool from my bad dreams and the earth it has
birthed beneath us

It is true that I left my fingernails full in the flesh of the cyclone amongst
the brawl of huge cockchafers
and even to making spurt a new yellow semen
throwing myself under its belly to measure
my rutting

Now
by the hard blood of rape
between two criminals
I know the hour
he who dies
he who leaves
But *one* but I
enclosed in the tuft that benumbs me
and by the grace of dogs
beneath the innocent and liana-unpleating wind
a hero of the hunt helmeted with a golden bird

.

La tornade

Le temps que
          le sénateur s'aperçut que la tornade était assise dans son
          assiette
          sur ses grosses fesses de betterave
          et les rondelles de saucisson de ses cuisses
          vicieusement croisées
et la tornade était dans l'air fourrageant dans Kansas-City
Le temps que
          le pasteur aperçut la tornade dans l'œil bleu de la femme du
          shériff
et la tornade fut dehors faisant apparaître à tous sa large face puant comme dix mille nègres entassés dans un train
le temps pour la tornade de s'esclaffer de rire dans le sexe d'une putain
et la tornade fit sur tout une jolie imposition de mains de ses belles mains blanches d'ecclésiastique
Le temps pour Dieu de s'apercevoir
          qu'il avait bu de trop cent verres de sang de bourreau
et la ville fut une fraternité de taches blanches et noires répandues en cadavres sur la peau d'un cheval abattu en plein galop
Le temps pour la tornade d'écrire un roman policier et la tornade coiffée de son chapeau cow-boy s'empare de lui en lui criant HAUT LES MAINS de la grande voix creuse dont Dieu se sert pour parler aux poules — et tout tremble
et la tornade tordit l'acier et les oiseaux tombaient foudroyés du ciel
Et la tornade ayant subi les provinces de la mémoire riche gravat des suppliciés craché d'un ciel engrangé de sentences tout trembla une seconde fois l'acier tordu fut retordu
Et la tornade qui avait avalé comme un vol de grenouilles son troupeau de toitures et de cheminées respira bruyamment une pensée que les prophètes n'avaient jamais su deviner

The Tornado

By the time that
          the senator noticed that the tornado was sitting in his plate
          on fat beet buttocks
          with the sliced sausage of its thighs
          lecherously crossed
the tornado was in the air foraging through Kansas City
By the time that
          the minister spotted the tornado in the blue eye of the
          sheriff's wife
it was outside displaying to everybody its huge face stinking like ten thousand
niggers crammed into a train
in the time it took for the tornado to guffaw into a whore's vagina
it performed over everything a nice laying-on-of-hands those beautiful white
clerical hands
In the time it took God to notice
          that he had drunk one hundred glasses of executioner blood
          too many
the city was a brotherhood of white and black spots scattered in cadavers on
the hide of a horse felled at full gallop
In the time it took for the tornado to write a detective novel the tornado
wearing its cowboy hat seized hold of it shouting HANDS UP in the
loud empty voice that God employs when speaking to chickens—and
everything trembles and the tornado twisted the steel and birds were falling
thunderstruck from the sky
And the tornado having suffered the provinces of the memory rich debris of
the executed
spat from a sky stored full of judgments everything trembled for a second
time the twisted steel was retwisted
And the tornado that had gobbled up like a flight of frogs its herd of roofs
and chimneys noisily exhaled a thought the prophets had never known how
to divine

Lynch II

Poings carnassiers teintés du ciel brisé
torche parmi les fûts héréditaires
œil sans rives sans mémoire
dieu et que n'importunent vos fumées bleues
par la mort et la fête
avec aux naseaux des fleurs inespérées
avec sur le dos le jeune vol de courlis des oiseaux de la phosphorescence
et un perfide chant vivant
dans les ruines indestructibles de son silence

Lynch II

Carnassial fists stained by a cracked sky
torch amidst the ancestral boles
eye without shores without memory
god and one that your blue fumes do not importune
by death and feasting
with in his nostrils unhoped-for flowers
with on his back the youthful flight of the curlew birds of phosphorescence
and a perfidious chant alive
in the indestructible ruins of his silence

Apothéose

À la quête de mes pas
dans la chaleur du temple mal circonscrit d'une cicatrice
cette distance qui toujours s'accroît
la mauvaise herbe de ma lumière
tout ce que j'ai pu ronger de mur (diaphragme à chaque point du jour que fait l'holothurie)

  minute il me tombera des pépites et des nids d'hirondelle
  il me tombera une vague de crotales et d'escarbilles
  il me tombera cet étui où je cache ma dent de sagesse
  ce paquet de feuilles qui m'empêche d'entendre dans le camouflage féroce de ma sueur indivise
  lorsque l'on gaule des noix dans les champs toujours bleus des terres importées par le déluge
  dans un semis de cloaques
  parmi les enfants de chœur de la moraine
  sous les dagues de nacre dont on marque les fronts et les cornes de l'éther
  qui chantent jusqu'aux prunelles

Il en tombera un gâteau de tsé-tsé pour le Te-Deum
une carcasse couchée dans le sable
une aigle impériale des menottes un collier de verroterie
il en tombera assez pour faire monter le cours de la Tamise
                et un cacatoès pour le pape
Il en tombera toujours quelque chose un indicateur de police un sacristain un poteau téléphonique un clou de girofle
Allons-y pour l'oraison d'une poussière de calcédoine pour la feuille morte pour la rive buissonnière d'un sang mal dissout pour les faunes réinventées à la mauvaise chandelle du tigre qui brûle tant bien que mal à partir de l'empreinte
                Il en tombera un hareng-saur

Pourquoi espèce de nom d'un scrupule ne pas faire suer et resuer le temps placide pour qu'il en tombe tous les pots de vin de notre sang sur la terre enfin saoûle
et la parole bien claire de son tonnerre

Apotheosis

In search of my steps
in the heat of the temple poorly circumscribed by a scar
this distance that always increases
the weed of my light
all I've been able to wear away of a wall (diaphragm the holothurian creates
at each daybreak)

hold on! nuggets and swallows' nests shall fall to me
a wave of rattlesnakes and clinkers shall fall to me
this case in which I hide my wisdom tooth shall fall to me
this bundle of leaves that keeps me from hearing in the ferocious camouflage
of my undivided sweat
when they thrash the walnut trees in the forever blue fields of lands imported
by the deluge
in a sowing of cesspools
among the child choristers of the moraine
under the mother-of-pearl daggers they use to mark the foreheads and the
horns of the ether singing in the sloes

A tsetse cake shall fall for the Te Deum
a carcass couched in sand
an imperial eagle handcuffs a necklace of glass beads
enough shall fall to make the level of the Thames rise
                              and a cockatoo for the pope
Something shall always fall a police informer a sacristan a telephone pole
a clove
Let's go for the prayer of chalcedony dust for the dead leaf for the bank
thicket of a badly dissolved blood for the fauna reinvented for that badly
candlelit tiger burning as best it can at the start of its tracks
                              A smoked herring shall fall

Why wretched name of a scruple not make placid time sweat and re-sweat
so that all our bribe-potted blood shall fall onto the finally drunken soil
and the truly clear word of its thunder

Croisade du Silence

Et maintenant
que les vastes oiseaux se suicident
que les entrailles des animaux noircissent sur le couteau du sacrifice que
les prêtres se plantent une vocation aux carrefours noués dans le terreau
du bric-à-brac
que dans les salles d'attente les cygnes mercuriels de la bielle lancés sur la
carte du vide
chantent
la stérilité s'exténue de ton être à plusieurs
sur ma main droite un animal chante
des dragons à ton être la main droite décompose ses semailles de ton être
à plusieurs la nécessité s'écroule de l'ignoble horizon

O Tombouctou à genoux dans les sables
O vision de la mer de nuages vers Cuba
O sous la neige de l'aube l'éclat de l'arroyo

lorsque dans tes venaisons une pierre comble à mille visages le grand trou
que dans tes chairs faisait l'eau sombre de la parole
l'éteint Chamborazo dévore encore le monde

Crusade of Silence

And now
that the enormous birds commit suicide
that animal entrails blacken on the sacrificial knife that priests stand firm
a calling at the crossroads knotted in the compost of bric-a-brac
that in waiting rooms the mercurial swans of the connecting-rod launched
onto the map of the void
sing
sterility is worked to death from your being several
on my right hand an animal sings
dragons to your being the right hand decomposes its sowings from your
being several necessity crumbles away from the ignoble horizon

O Timbuktu on its knees in the sand
O vision of the sea of clouds toward Cuba
O under the dawn snow the sparkling arroyo

when in your venisons a stone blocks with a thousand faces the great hole
made in your flesh by the saturnine water of the word
extinct Chimborazo still devours the world

Totem

De loin en proche de proche en loin le sistre des circoncis et un soleil hors mœurs
buvant dans la gloire de ma poitrine un grand coup de vin rouge et de mouches
comment d'étage en étage de détresse en héritage le totem ne bondirait-il pas au sommet des buildings sa tiédeur de cheminée et de trahison ?
comme la distraction salée de ta langue destructrice
comme le vin de ton venin
comme ton rire de dos de marsouin dans l'argent du naufrage
comme la souris verte qui naît de la belle eau captive de tes paupières
comme la course des gazelles de sel fin de la neige sur la tête sauvage des femmes et de l'abîme
comme les grandes étamines de tes lèvres dans le filet bleu du continent
comme l'éclatement de feu de la minute dans la trame serrée du temps
comme la chevelure de genêt qui s'obstine à pousser dans l'arrière-saison de tes yeux à marine
chevaux du quadrige piétinez la savane de ma parole vaste ouverte

du blanc au fauve
il y a les sanglots le silence la mer rouge et la nuit

Totem

From far to near from near to far the circumciseds' sistrum and a sun outside
principles
drinking in the glory of my chest a big slug of red wine and flies
how from tier to tier from distress to heritage would the totem not leap its
tepidity of smokestack and treason to the top of the office complex?
like the salty inadvertence of your destructive tongue
like the wine of your venom
like your porpoise-back laughter in the silver of the shipwreck
like the green mouse born of the beautiful captive water of your eyelids
like the flight of gazelles of fine salt of snow over the wild heads of the
women and of the abyss
like the broad stamens of your lips in the continent's blue net
like the rifle crack of the minute in the tightened woof of time
like the gorse chevelure that stubbornly grows in the off-season of your
marine eyes
quadriga horses stamp the savanna of my vast open speech

from white to fawn
there are sobs silence the red sea and the night

Défaire et refaire le soleil

demeure faite d'on ne sait à quel saint se vouer
demeure faite d'éclats de sabre
demeure faite de cous tranchés
demeure faite de grains de la pluie du déluge
demeure faite d'harmonicas mâles
demeure faite d'eau verte et d'ocarinas femelles
demeure faite de plumes d'ange déchu
demeure faite de touffes de petits rires
demeure faite de cloches d'alarme
demeure faite de peaux de bêtes et de paupières
demeure faite de grains de senevé
demeure faite de doigts d'éventails
demeure faite de masse d'armes
demeure faite d'une pluie de petits cils
demeure faite d'une épidémie de tambours

quel visage aurions-nous à ne pas défier la mer d'un pied plus retentissant que nos cœurs à grenouilles

Demeure faite de crotte de poule
demeure faite de sumac toxique
demeure faite de plumes pour couronne d'oiseau-mouche

Geôlier est-ce que vous ne voyez pas que mon œil toujours serré dans mes poings crie que mon estomac me remonte à la gorge et l'aliment d'un vol de ravets nés de sa mouture de saburre ?

Belle ange intime usure la mienne la vôtre le pardon est un pied-plat à bannir de notre vue mais ma colère m'apporte seule le bouquet de votre odeur et sa poignée de clés.

Puissant d'elle naissez comme d'elle je nais au jour.

Geôlier mes poings serrés, m'y voici, mes poings serrés m'y voilà dans ma demeure à votre barbe.

Unmaking and Remaking the Sun

dwelling made of not knowing which way to turn
dwelling made of saber glitter
dwelling made of cut necks
dwelling made of rainstorms of the deluge
dwelling made of male harmonicas
dwelling made of green water and female ocarinas
dwelling made of fallen angel feathers
dwelling made of the wisps of little laughs
dwelling made of alarm bells
dwelling made of animal skins and eyelids
dwelling made of mustard seeds
dwelling made of fan fingers
dwelling made of a mace
dwelling made of a rain of little eyelashes
dwelling made of an epidemic of drums

what would we look like on not defying the sea with a step more resounding than our froglike hearts

Dwelling made of chicken droppings
dwelling made of poison sumac
dwelling made of feathers for a hummingbird crown

Jailer don't you see that my eye forever clenched in my fists cries out that my stomach once again rises to my throat and feeds it a swarm of roaches born of its milled saburra?

Beautiful angel intimate usury mine yours forgiveness is a toady to be banned from our sight but my anger alone brings me the bouquet of your odor and its fistful of keys.

Powerful of her be born as of her I am born at daybreak.

Jailer my fists clenched, here I am, my fists clenched there I am in my dwelling in your face.

Demeure faite de votre impuissance de la puissance de mes gestes simples de la liberté de mes spermatozoïdes demeure matrice noire tendue de courtine rouge le seul reposoir que je bénisse d'où je peux regarder le monde éclater au choix de mon silence

Dwelling made of your impotence of the power of my simple acts of the freedom of my spermatozoa dwelling black womb hung with a red curtain sole altar I may bless while watching the world explode at the option of my silence

Samba

Tout ce qui d'anse s'est agglutiné pour former tes seins toutes les cloches d'hibiscus toutes les huîtres perlières toutes les pistes brouillées qui forment une mangrove tout ce qu'il y a de soleil en réserve dans les lézards de la sierra tout ce qu'il faut d'iode pour faire un jour marin tout ce qu'il faut de nacre pour dessiner un bruit de conque sous-marine
Si tu voulais
     les tétrodons à la dérive iraient se donnant la main
Si tu voulais
     tout le long du jour les péronias de leurs queues feraient des routes et
     les évêques seraient si rares qu'on ne serait pas surpris d'apprendre
     qu'ils ont été avalés par les crosses de trichomans
Si tu voulais
     la force psychique
     assurerait toute seule la nuit d'un balisage d'araras
Si tu voulais
     dans les faubourgs qui furent pauvres les norias remonteraient avec
     dans les godets le parfum des bruits les plus neufs dont se grise la terre
     dans ses plis infernaux
Si tu voulais
     les fauves boiraient aux fontaines
     et dans nos têtes
     les patries de terre violente
     tendraient comme un doigt aux oiseaux l'allure sans secousse des
     hauts mélèzes

Samba

All that from a cove combined to form your breasts all the hibiscus bells all the pearl oysters all the jumbled tracks that form a mangrove all the sun that is stored in sierra lizards all the iodine needed to make a marine day all the mother-of-pearl needed to delineate the sound of a submarine conch
If you wanted them to
      the drifting tetraodons would move hand in hand
If you wanted them to
      all day long phoronids would make roads with their tentacles and
      bishops would be so rare it would not be surprising to hear that they
      had been swallowed by the bristle ferns' crosiers
If you wanted it to
      psychic force
      would on its own mark out the night with macaw buoys
If you wanted them to
      in formerly poor suburbs norias would draw up in their scoops the
      perfume of the newest sounds with which the earth intoxicates itself in
      its infernal folds
If you wanted them to
      wild beasts would drink from the fountains
      and in our heads
      the violent earth homelands
      would extend like a finger to the birds the joltless bearing of high
      larches

Intercesseur

Bond vague de l'once sans garrot
au zénith
poussière de lait
un midi est avec moi
glissé très rare de tes haras
d'ombres cuites et
très rares entrelacs des doigts
O soleil déchiré
aveugle paon magique et frais
aux mains d'arches d'éprouvettes
futile éclipse de l'espace

Intercessor

Wavering bound of the garrotless snow leopard
to the zenith
milky dust
a midday is with me
slipped away very rare from your stud farms
of cooked shadows and
very rare interlocking of fingers
O torn sun
blind peacock magical and cool
with arched test tube hands
futile eclipse of space

La roue

La roue est la plus belle découverte de l'homme et la seule
il y a le soleil qui tourne
il y a la terre qui tourne
il y a ton visage qui tourne sur l'essieu de ton cou quand tu pleures mais
vous minutes n'enroulerez-vous pas sur la bobine à vivre le sang lapé
l'art de souffrir aiguisé comme les moignons d'arbre par les couteaux
de l'hiver
la biche saoule de ne pas boire
qui me pose sur la margelle inattendue ton
visage de goélette démâtée
ton visage
comme un village endormi au fond d'un lac
et qui renaît au jour de l'herbe et de l'année
germe

The Wheel

The wheel is man's most beautiful and sole discovery
there is the sun that turns
there is the earth that turns
there is your face turning on the axle of your neck when you weep
but you minutes won't you wind on the spindle for living the lapped up blood
the art of suffering sharpened like tree stumps by the knives of winter
the doe intoxicated from not drinking
that on the unexpected well curb presents me with your
face of a dismasted schooner
your face
like a village asleep at the bottom of a lake
and which is reborn to daylight from the grass and from the year
germinates

Calme

Le temps bien sûr sera nul du péché
les portes céderont sous l'assaut des eaux
les orchidées pousseront leur douce tête violente de torturé à travers la
claire-voie que deux à deux font les paroles
les lianes dépêcheront du fond de leurs veilles une claire batterie de sangsues
dont l'embrassade sera de la force irrésistible des parfums
de chaque grain de sable naîtra un oiseau
de chaque fleur simple sortira un scorpion (tout étant recomposé)
les trompettes des droseras éclateront pour marquer l'heure où abdiquer
mes épaisses lèvres plantées d'aiguilles en faveur de l'armature flexible des
futurs aloès
l'émission de chair naïve autour de la douleur sera généralisée hors de tout
rapport avec l'incursion bivalve des cestodes
cependant que les hirondelles nées de ma salive agglutineront avec les algues
apportées par les vagues qui montent de toi
le mythe sanglant d'une minute jamais murmurée

aux étages des tours du silence les vautours s'envoleront avec au bec
des lambeaux de la vieille chair trop peu calme pour nos squelettes

Calm

Time shall of course be void of sin
gates shall buckle under the assault of waters
orchids shall push their sweet violent torture-victim heads through the
openwork that words form two by two
lianas shall dispatch from the depth of their vigils a luminous battery
of leeches whose embrace shall have the irresistible force of perfumes
from each grain of sand a bird shall be born
from each simple flower a scorpion shall emerge (everything being
compound)
the droseras' trumpets shall blast to mark the hour for abdicating my thick
needle-implanted lips in favor of the flexible armature of future aloes
the emission of naïve flesh around pain shall be generalized outside of any
relationship with the bivalvular incursion of cestodes
while the swallows born of my saliva shall agglutinate with the algae carried
by the waves that rise from you
the bloody myth of a never murmured moment

on the platforms of the towers of silence the vultures shall take flight, in their
beaks shreds of old flesh too uncalm for our skeletons

An neuf

       Les hommes ont taillé dans leurs tourments une fleur
       qu'ils ont juchée sur les hauts plateaux de leur face
       la faim leur fait un dais
       une image se dissout dans leur dernière larme
       ils ont bu jusqu'à l'horreur féroce
       les monstres rythmés par les écumes
En ce temps-là
il y eut une
inoubliable
métamorphose
       les chevaux ruaient un peu de rêve sur leurs sabots
       de gros nuages d'incendie s'arrondirent en champignon
       sur toutes les places publiques
       ce fut une peste merveilleuse
       sur le trottoir les moindres réverbères tournaient leur tête
       de phare
       quant à l'avenir anophèle vapeur brûlante il sifflait dans les jardins
En ce temps-là
le mot ondée
et le mot sol meuble
le mot aube
et le mot copeaux
conspirèrent pour la première fois
       Des forêts naquirent aux borinages
       et des péniches sur les canaux de l'air
       et du salpêtre rouge des blessés sur le pavé
       il naquit des arums au-delà des fillettes
Ce fut l'année où les germes de l'homme se choisirent dans l'homme
le tendre pas d'un cœur nouveau

New Year

        Out of their torments men carved a flower
        that they perched on the high plateaus of their faces
        hunger makes a canopy for them
        an image dissolves in their last tear
        they drank foam-rhythmed monsters
        to the point of ferocious horror
In those days
there was an
unforgettable
metamorphosis
        on their hooves horses were kicking a bit of dream
        fat fiery clouds filled out like mushrooms
        all over the public squares
        there was a marvelous pestilence
        on the sidewalks the faintest streetlamps were rotating their
        lighthouse heads
        as for the anophelic future in the gardens it was hissing a
        scorching vapor
In those days
the word shower
and the word friable soil
the word dawn
and the word woodchips
conspired for the first time
        Forests were born in the Borinage
        and barges on the canals of the air
        and from the red saltpeter of those wounded on the pavement
        were born arums beyond young girls
That was the year when the seeds of humankind chose within man the tender
approach of a new heart

Ex-voto pour un naufrage

Hélé helélé le Roi est un grand roi
que sa majesté daigne regarder dans mon anus pour voir s'il contient des
diamants
que sa majesté daigne explorer ma bouche pour voir combien elle contient
de carats
tam-tam ris
tam-tam ris
je porte la litière du roi
j'étends le tapis du roi
je suis le tapis du roi
je porte les écrouelles du roi
je suis le parasol du roi
riez riez tam-tams des kraals
tam-tams des mines qui riez sous cape
tam-tams sacrés qui riez à la barbe des missionnaires de vos dents de rat
et d'hyène
tam-tams de salut qui vous foutez de toutes les armées du salut
tam-tams de la forêt
      tam-tams du désert
           noire encore vierge que chaque pierre murmure
à l'insu du désastre—ma fièvre
tam-tam pleure
tam-tam pleure
tam-tam bas
tam-tam bas
brûlé jusqu'au fougueux silence de nos pleurs sans rivage
tam-tam bas
      plus bas oreille considérable
(les oreilles rouges—les oreilles—loin ont la fatigue vite)
tam-tam bas
roulez bas rien qu'un temps de bille pour les oreilles loin
      sans parole sans fin sans astre
le pur temps de charbon de nos longues affres majeures
roulez roulez lourds roulez bas tam-tams délires sans vocable lions roux sans
crinière défilés de la soif puanteurs des marigots le soir
tam-tams qui protégez mes trois âmes mon cerveau mon cœur mon foie
tam-tams durs qui très haut maintenez ma demeure
d'eau de vent d'iode d'étoiles

Ex-Voto for a Shipwreck

Hélé helélé the King is a great king
let his majesty deign to look up my anus to see if it contains diamonds
let his majesty deign to explore my mouth to see how many carats it
contains
laugh tom-tom
laugh tom-tom
I carry the king's litter
I roll out the king's carpet
I am the king's carpet
I carry the king's scrofula
I am the king's parasol
laugh laugh tom-toms of the kraals
tom-toms of the mines laughing beneath their cape
sacred tom-toms laughing about your rat and hyena teeth under the very nose
of the missionaries
tom-toms of salvation who don't give a damn about all the salvation armies
tom-toms of the forest
      tom-toms of the desert
      black still virginal muttered by each stone
unbeknownst to the disaster—my fever
weep tom-tom
weep tom-tom
soft tom-tom
soft tom-tom
burned down to the impetuous silence of our shoreless tears
soft tom-tom
      softer still substantial ear
(red ears—ears—distantly the rapid fatigue)
soft tom-tom
roll soft no faster than a log for distant ears
      without utterance without purpose without star
the pure carbon duration of our endless major pangs
roll roll deep roll soft tom-toms speechless deliriums russet lions without
manes processions of thirst stench of the backwaters at night
tom-toms that protect my three souls my brain my heart my liver
harsh tom-toms that maintain on high my dwelling
of water of wind of iodine of stars

sur le roc foudroyé de ma tête noire
et toi tam-tam frère pour qui il m'arrive de garder tout le long du jour un mot
tour à tour chaud et frais dans ma bouche comme le goût peu connu de la
vengeance
tam-tams de kalaari
tam-tams de Bonne-Espérance qui coiffez le cap de vos menaces
O tam-tam du Zululand
Tam-tam de Chaka
tam tam tam
tam tam tam
Roi nos montagnes sont des cavales en rut saisies en pleine convulsion
de mauvais sang
Roi nos plaines sont des rivières qu'impatientent les fournitures de
pourritures montées de la mer et de vos caravelles
Roi nos pierres sont des lampes ardentes d'une espérance veuve de dragon
Roi nos arbres sont la forme déployée que prend une flamme trop grosse
pour notre cœur trop faible pour un donjon
Riez riez donc tam-tams de Cafrerie
comme le beau point d'interrogation du scorpion
dessiné au pollen sur le tableau du ciel et de nos cervelles à minuit
comme un frisson de reptile marin charmé par la pensée du mauvais temps
du petit rire renversé de la mer dans les hublots très beaux du naufrage

over the blasted rock of my black head
and you brother tom-tom for whom sometimes all day long I keep a word
now hot now cool in my mouth like the little-known taste of vengeance
tom-toms of kalahari
tom-toms of Good Hope capping the cape with your threats
O tom-tom of Zululand
Tom-tom of Shaka
tom tom tom
tom tom tom
King our mountains are mares in heat caught in the full convulsion of
bad blood
King our plains are rivers vexed by the rotting provisions drifting in from
the sea and from your caravels
King our stones are lamps burning with a dragon widow hope
King our trees are the unfurled shape taken by a flame too big for our hearts
too weak for a dungeon
Laugh laugh then tom-toms of Kaffirland
like the scorpion's beautiful question mark
drawn in pollen on the canvas of the sky and of our brains at midnight
like the shiver of a sea reptile charmed by the anticipation of bad weather
of the little upside-down laugh of the sea in the sunken ship's gorgeous
portholes

Depuis Akkad depuis Élam depuis Sumer

Maître des trois chemins, tu as en face de toi un homme qui a beaucoup marché.
Maître des trois chemins, tu as en face de toi un homme qui a marché sur les mains marché sur les pieds marché sur le ventre marché sur le cul.
Depuis Elam. Depuis Akkad. Depuis Sumer.
Maître des trois chemins, tu as en face de toi un homme qui a beaucoup porté.
Et de vrai mes amis j'ai porté j'ai porté depuis Elam, depuis Akkad, depuis Sumer.
J'ai porté le corps du commandant. J'ai porté le chemin de fer du commandant. J'ai porté la locomotive du commandant le coton du commandant. J'ai porté sur ma tête laineuse qui se passe si bien de coussinet Dieu, la machine, la route — le Dieu du commandant.
Maître des trois chemins j'ai porté sous le soleil, j'ai porté dans le brouillard j'ai porté sur les tessons de braise des fourmis manians. J'ai porté le parasol j'ai porté l'explosif j'ai porté le carcan et comme sur les rives du Nil on voit dans la vase molle le pied juste de l'ibis j'ai laissé partout sur les berges sur les montagnes sur les rivages le grigri de mes pieds à carcans.
Depuis Akkad. Depuis Elam. Depuis Sumer.
Maître des trois chemins. Maîtres des trois rigoles plaise que pour une fois — la première depuis Akkad depuis Elam depuis Sumer — le museau plus tanné apparemment que le cal de mes pieds mais en réalité plus doux que le bec minutieux du corbeau et comme drapé surnaturellement des plis amers que me fait ma grise peau d'emprunt (livrée que les hommes m'imposent chaque hiver) j'avance à travers les feuilles mortes de mon petit pas sorcier

vers là où menace triomphalement l'inépuisable injonction des hommes jetés aux ricanements noueux de l'ouragan. Depuis Elam depuis Akkad depuis Sumer.

All the Way from Akkad, from Elam, from Sumer

Master of the three paths, you have before you a man who has walked a lot.
Master of the three paths, you have before you a man who has walked on his hands on his feet on his belly on his backside.
All the way from Elam. From Akkad. From Sumer.
Master of the three paths, you have before you a man who has carried a lot. And truly my friends I have carried I have carried all the way from Elam, from Akkad, from Sumer.
I have carried the commandant's body. I have carried the commandant's railroad. I have carried the commandant's locomotive, the commandant's cotton. I have carried on my nappy head that gets along just fine without a little cushion God, the machine, the road—the commandant's God.
Master of the three paths I have carried under the sun, I have carried in the mist I have carried over the ember shards of legionary ants. I have carried the parasol I have carried the explosives I have carried the iron collar and as on the shores of the Nile you see in the soft mud the just foot of the ibis I have left everywhere on the banks on the mountains on the shores the gri-gri of my cancan feet.
All the way from Akkad. From Elam. From Sumer.
Master of the three paths, Master of the three channels, may it please you for once—the first time since Akkad since Elam since Sumer—my muzzle apparently more tanned than the calluses on my feet but in reality softer than the crow's scrupulous beak and as if draped supernaturally in bitter folds provided by my borrowed gray skin (a livery men force onto me every winter)—that I may advance through the dead leaves with my little sorcerer steps

toward where the inexhaustible injunction of men thrown to the knotted sneers of the hurricane threatens triumphantly. All the way from Elam from Akkad from Sumer.

Au serpent

Il m'est arrivé dans l'effarement des villes de chercher quel animal adorer.
Alors je remontais aux temps premiers. En défaisant les cycles en délaçant les nœuds en brisant les intrigues en enlevant les couvertures en tuant mes otages je cherchais.
Fouineur. Tapir. Déracineur.
Où où où l'animal qui m'avertissait des crues
Où où où l'oiseau qui me guidait au miel
Où où où l'oiseau qui me divulguait les sources
le souvenir de grandes alliances trahies de grandes amitiés perdues par notre faute m'exaltait
Où où où
Où où où
La parole me fut vulgaire
O serpent dos somptueux enfermes-tu dans ton onduleuse lanière l'âme puissante de mon grand-père ?
Salut à toi serpent par qui le matin agite la belle chevelure mauve des manguiers de décembre et pour qui la nuit invention du lait dégringole de son mur ses souris lumineuses
Salut à toi serpent cannelé comme le fond de la mer et que mon cœur nous détache de vrai comme prémisse du déluge
Salut à toi serpent ta reptation est plus majestueuse que *leur* démarche et la paix que leur Dieu ne donne pas tu la détiens souverainement.

Serpent délire et paix
la campagne me démembre sur les claies d'un vent d'outrage les secrets qui firent retentir leurs pas au débouché de la trappe millénaire des gorges qu'ils serraient à étrangler.

à la poubelle ! que tous croupissent à composer la banderolle d'un corbeau noir s'affaiblissant en un battement d'ailes blanches.
Serpent
dégoût large et royal accablant le retour dans les sables de l'imposture embrun qui nourrit le ras vain de la mouette
à la tempête pâle des silences rassurants tu te chauffes le moins frêle.
Tu te baignes en deçà des cris les plus discords sur les écumes songeuses de l'herbe
quand le feu s'exhale de la barque veuve qui consume le cap de l'éclat
de l'écho

To the Serpent

I have had occasion in the bewilderment of cities to search for the right animal to adore. So I worked my way back to the first times. Undoing cycles untying knots crushing plots removing covers killing my hostages I searched.
Pryer. Tapir. Uprooter.
Where where where the animal who warned me of floods
Where where where the bird who led me to honey
Where where where the bird who revealed to me the fountainheads
the memory of great alliances betrayed great friendships lost through our fault exalted me
Where where where
Where where where
The word made vulgar to me
O serpent sumptuous back do you enclose in your sinuous lash the powerful soul of my grandfather?
Greetings to you serpent through whom morning shakes its beautiful mango mauve December chevelure and for whom the milk-invented night tumbles its luminous mice down its wall
Greetings to you serpent grooved like the bottom of the sea and which my heart truly unbinds for us like a premise of the deluge
Greetings to you serpent your reptation is more majestic than *their* gait and the peace their God gives not you hold supremely.

Serpent delirium and peace
over the hurdles of a scurrilous wind the countryside dismembers for me
secrets whose steps resounded at the opening of the millenary throat trap
they tightened to strangulation.

to the trashcan! may they all rot in portraying the banner of a black crow weakening in a beating of white wings.
Serpent
broad and royal disgust overpowering the return in the sands of deception spindrift nourishing the vain raft of the seagull
in the pale tempest of reassuring silences you warm the least frail of yourself.
You bathe yourself this side of the most discordant cries on dreamy spumes of grass
when fire is exhaled from the widow boat that consumes the cape of the echo's flash

mais pour mieux faire frissonner de tes morts successives—fréquentation verte des éléments—ta menace.

Ta menace oui ta menace corps issant des brumes rauques de l'amertume où il a corrompu le soucieux gardien de phare et qui siffle et prend son petit temps de galop vers les rayons assassins de la découverte.

Serpent
charmant piqueur du sein des femmes et par qui la mort s'insinue maturité au fond d'un fruit seul seigneur seigneur seul dont la multiple image fait sur l'autel du figuier maudit une offrande de chevelure qui est une menace de poulpe qui est une main sagace qui ne pardonne pas aux lâches

just to make your successive deaths shiver all the more—green frequenting of the elements—your threat.

Your threat yes your threat body issuant from the raucous haze of bitterness where it corrupted the concerned lighthouse keeper and that hisses and takes its little gallop time toward the assassin rays of discovery.

Serpent
charming biter of womens' breasts and through whom death steals into the maturity in the depths of a fruit sole lord lord alone whose multiple image places on the altar of the strangler fig an offering of chevelure that is an octopodal threat that is a sagacious hand that does not pardon cowards

Torture

Tous ceux dont le cœur est une tache d'encre sur le cahier d'un enfant
tous ceux dont la parole est une étreinte brisée dans un dernier effort de
gigantisme terrestre
portent soit sur les mains une lune striée par le frottement des moraines
de glacier soit dans la démarche un mauvais serpent qui à titre initiatoire
traverse un zèbre de cercles et d'ellipses
Tous ceux qui savent dessiner sur la pourpre impériale de grandes taches
de sperme sombre accompagnées du diagramme de leur chute
tous ceux dont les doigts sont une somptuosité inédite de papillons courbés
selon l'axe de la terre
O tous ceux dont le regard est un carrousel d'oiseaux nés d'un équilibre
surhumain d'éponges et de fragments de galaxie éteinte sous le talon d'une
petite gare

Torture

All those whose hearts are an inkblot in a child's copybook all those whose word is an embrace broken in a final effort of terrestrial gigantism
either manifesting on their hands a moon scored by the friction of glacial moraines or showing in their gait an evil serpent that by right of initiation crosses a zebra of circles and ellipses
All those who know how to show on imperial purple great blots of dark sperm accompanied by a diagram of their fall
all those whose fingers are an unprecedented sumptuousness of butterflies curved according to the earth's axis
O all those whose gaze is a carousel of birds born of a superhuman balance of sponges and of fragments from a galaxy extinguished beneath a small railway station's heel

Fanion

À Séville le front percé d'un œilleton du dernier taureau
au pôle le soleil purulent du noir
dans le fjord l'étranglement d'un râle
dans ma gorge le refus de passer d'un verre d'eau fraîche
Seigneur bourreau
pour l'amour du seigneur
donnez-moi un petit coup de dent d'hyène
au nom de l'humanité donnez-moi un petit coup de pied
au nom du fils comme du père empoisonnez le pavillon de mon oreille
car de toi sombre brigand Almamy Samory c'est à cheval que je vois ton image—vieillard et battant contre le flanc de la forêt natale et l'éclat du dernier continent
l'ultime hoquet d'un vouloir jeune et rude

Pennant

In Seville the peep-sight pierced forehead of the last bull
at the pole the purulent sun of blackness
in the fjord the strangulation of a death rattle
in my throat refusing to go down a glass of cool water
Lord executioner
for the love of the lord
give me a little hyena bite
in the name of humanity give me a little kick
in the name of the son as well as the father poison the pinna of my ear
for you sombre brigand Almamy Samory it is on horseback that I see
your image—an old man struggling with the forest's native flank and the
splintering of the last continent
the final hiccup of a will young and uncouth

À l'Afrique
à Wifredo Lam

Paysan frappe le sol de ta daba
dans le sol il y a une hâte que la syllabe de l'événement ne dénoue pas
je me souviens de la fameuse peste qui aura lieu en l'an 3000
il n'y avait pas eu d'étoile annoncière
mais seulement la terre en un flot sans galet pétrissant d'espace un pain d'herbe et de réclusion
frappe paysan frappe
le premier jour les oiseaux mourront
le second jour les poissons échouèrent
le troisième jour les animaux sortirent des bois
et faisaient aux villes une grande ceinture chaude très forte
frappe le sol de ta daba
il y a dans le sol la carte des transmutations et des ruses de la mort
le quatrième jour la végétation se fana
et tout tourna à l'aigre de l'agave à l'acacia
en aigrettes en orgues végétales
où le vent épineux jouait des flûtes et des odeurs tranchantes
Frappe paysan frappe
il naît au ciel des fenêtres qui sont mes yeux giclés
et dont la herse dans ma poitrine fait le rempart d'une ville qui refuse
de donner la passe aux muletiers de la désespérance
Frappe le sol de ta daba
il y a les eaux élémentaires qui chantent dans les virages du circuit magnétique l'éclosion des petits souliers de la terre
attente passementerie de lamproies j'attends d'une attente vulnéraire une campagne qui naîtra aux oreilles de ma compagne et verdira à son sexe
le ventre de ma compagne c'est le coup de tonnerre du beau temps
les cuisses de ma compagne jouent les arbres tombés le long de sa démarche
il y a au pied de nos châteaux-de-fées pour la rencontre du sang et du paysage
la salle de bal où des nains braquant leurs miroirs écoutent dans les plis de la pierre ou du sel croître le sexe du regard
paysan pour que débouche de la tête de la montagne celle que blesse le vent
pour que tiédisse dans sa gorge une gorgée de cloches
qui se parfilent en corbeaux en jupes en perceuses d'isthmes
pour que ma vague se dévore en sa vague et nous ramène sur le sable en noyés
en chair de goyaves déchirés en une main d'épure en belles algues en graine

To Africa
For Wifredo Lam

Peasant strike the soil with your pick hoe
in the soil there is an urgency no syllable of the event may unknot
I recall the notorious plague to occur in the year 3000
there was no annunciatory star
merely the earth in a pebbleless wave kneading out of space a bread of grass
and reclusion
strike peasant strike
on the first day the birds shall die
on the second day the fish beached
on the third day the animals came out of the woods
and formed a hot belt great and powerful around the cities
strike the soil with your pick hoe
there is in the soil the map of the transmutations and trickeries of death
on the fourth day the vegetation withered
and everything turned bitter from the agave to the acacia
into egrets into vegetal organ pipes
or the spiny wind played flutes and trenchant odors
Strike peasant strike
in the sky are born windows that are my spurted eyes
and their harrow in my chest forms the rampart of a city refusing passage
to the muleteers of despair
Strike the soil with your pick hoe
there are elemental waters singing in the bends of the magnetic circuit
the hatching of the earth's little shoes
passemented lamprey expectation I await with vulnerary expectations a
countryside to be born in my mistress's ears and to turn verdant in her sex
the belly of my mistress is a thunderbolt of fine weather
the thighs of my mistress play at being trees fallen along her stride
there is at the foot of our fairy castles for the rendezvous of blood and
landscape the ballroom in which dwarfs brandishing mirrors listen to the sex
of a gaze growing in the folds of stone or salt
peasant so that she whom the wind wounds can emerge from the mountain's
head
so that a mouthful of bells can cool down in her throat
bells that unravel into crows into skirts into drillers of isthmuses
so that my wave may be devoured in her wave and lead us back onto the sand
as drowned ones as the flesh of guavas torn into the blueprint of a hand

volante en bulle en souvenance en arbre précatoire
soit ton geste une vague qui hurle et se reprend vers le creux de rocs aimés
comme pour parfaire une île rebelle à naître
il y a dans le sol demain en scrupule et la parole à charger aussi bien que
le silence
et j'emmerde ceux qui ne comprennent pas qu'il n'est pas beau de louer
l'éternel et de célébrer ton nom ô Très-Haut
car tu n'as ni la force luisante du buffle ni la science mathématique de l'ibis
ni la patience du nègre
et la bouse de vache que tu roules avec moins d'adresse que le scarabée
le cède en luxe aux mots noués sous ma langue

Éternel je ne pense pas à toi ni à tes chauves-souris
mais je pense à Ishtar mal défendue par la meute friable de ses robes que
chaque parole zéro des luettes plus bas vers où feignent de dormir les métaux
avec leur face encline
et les serpents qui balancent au fond de nos exils des cheveux de sycomore
enchiffre d'ombre et de connaissance

Paysan le vent où glissent des carènes arrête autour de mon visage la main
lointaine d'un songe
ton champ dans son saccage éclate debout de monstres marins
que je n'ai garde d'écarter
et mon geste est pur autant qu'un front d'oubli

frappe paysan je suis ton fils
à l'heure du soleil qui se couche le crépuscule sous ma paupière clapote vert
jaune et tiède d'iguanes inassoupis
mais la belle autruche courrière qui subitement naît des formes émues de la
femme me fait de l'avenir les signes de l'amitié

into beautiful seaweed into aerial seed into a bubble into recollection into a precatory tree
let your act be a wave that howls and regathers toward the hollow of beloved rocks as if to perfect an island rebelling against birth
there is in the soil the scruple of tomorrow and the burden of speech as well as of silence
and to hell with those who do not understand that it is not beautiful to praise the eternal and to celebrate your name o Most High
for you have neither the glistening strength of the buffalo nor the mathematical science of the ibis nor the patience of the black man
and the cow-dung that you roll with less dexterity than the scarab is second in luxury to the words knotted beneath my tongue

Eternal I am thinking neither of you nor of your bats
but I do think of Ishtar badly defended by the crumbling hound-pack of her vestments whom each zero utterance of uvulas further below near metals pretending to sleep with their faces inclines
and the serpents swaying sycamore hair in the depth of our exiles enciphers with shadow and knowledge

Peasant the wind in which ship hulls glide stops the distant hand of a dream around my face
your field in its havoc explodes erect with deep-sea monsters that I shall not thrust aside
and my gesture is as pure as a forgetful brow

strike peasant I am your son
at the hour of the setting sun dusk splashes under my eyelid a yellowish green tepid with undozing iguanas
but the beautiful messenger ostrich born suddenly from the aroused forms of woman beckons to me of the future in friendship

Délicatesse d'une momie

J'ai embaumé ma tête coupée dans une peau très mince
dont il faudrait calculer le pouvoir d'absorption
vers ? fil ? des langes ? à l'autre bout banquises ou anges
Regarde je suis si lisse qu'on croirait qu'on ne m'a jamais regardé
certes j'ai échappé aux chiens
est-ce pour rien
il y a les sirènes qui sonnent l'appel des villes
les hommes qui n'attendent pas les sapeurs du néant
et les prêtres interdits qui tout bas rient
Astrologues
toutes vos mesures sont dans ma démesure
          en coudées pyramidales
          en capacité de pleurer de respirer
et la caverne que la lourdeur de mes pas dessine est toujours face à toute
étoile polaire
Pas d'adieu (hispide est ma langue)
un grand oiseau est à mon chevet assis il a daigné me renverser la phrase
et l'horrible festin tout loin
mon geste bien arrimé
minute laps de parallaxe
la terre comme un bloc de glace en urine se disloque
et de l'innocente dérive de son écho alimente un béryl

Delicacy of a Mummy

I embalmed my severed head in a very thin skin
whose power of absorption would need to be calculated
worms? thread? swaddling clothes? at the other end ice floes or angels
Look I am so smooth you would think nobody had ever looked at me
of course I escaped the dogs
was that for nought
there are sirens that sound the call of cities
men who do not wait for the sappers of nothingness
and bewildered priests who laugh quietly
Astrologers
all your moderation is in my immoderation
            in pyramidal cubits
              in the capacity of weeping of breathing
and the cavern that the heaviness of my steps sketches is always facing every
pole star
No goodbye (hispid is my tongue)
a great bird is seated at my bedside it deigned to reverse for me the phrase
and the horrible so distant feast
my well-stowed gesture
minute lapse of parallax
the earth like a block of ice in urine breaks up
and from the innocent drift of its echo nourishes a beryl

Démons

Je frappai ses jambes et ses bras. Ils devinrent des pattes de fer terminées par des serres très puissantes recouvertes de petites plumes souples et vertes qui leur faisaient une gaine discernable mais très bien étudiée. D'une idée-à-peur de mon cerveau lui naquit son bec, d'un poisson férocement armé. Et l'animal fut devant moi oiseau. Son pas régulier comme une horloge arpentait despotiquement le sable rouge comme mesureur d'un champ sacré né de la larme perfide d'un fleuve. Sa tête ? je la vis très vite de verre translucide à travers lequel l'œil tournait un agencement de rouages très fins de poulies de bielles qui de temps en temps avec le jeu très impressionnant des pistons injectaient le temps de chrome et de mercure
Mais déjà la bête était sur moi.
Hélas elle était invulnérable.
Au dessous des seins et sur tout le ventre au dessous du cou et sur tout le dos ce que l'on prenait à première vue pour des plumes étaient des lamelles de fer peint qui lorsque l'animal ouvrait et refermait les ailes pour se secouer de la pluie et du sang faisaient une perspective que rien ne pouvait compromettre de relents et de bruits de cuillers heurtées par les mains blanches d'un séisme dans les corbeilles sordides d'un été trop malsain.

Demons

I struck its legs and its arms. They became iron paws ending in very powerful claws covered with supple little green feathers providing them with a noticeable but well-designed sheath. A fear-thought in my brain spawned its beak, as of a ferociously armed fish. And the animal was before me a bird. Its step regular as clockwork despotically paced the red sand like the surveyor of a sacred field born of a river's perfidious tear. Its head? in a flash, I saw it as translucid glass through which the eye turned fittings of intricate gears of pulleys of connecting-rods that now and then injected time with chrome and mercury through a quite impressive play of pistons
But the beast was already upon me.
Alas it was invulnerable.
Beneath its breasts and all over its belly beneath its neck and all over its back what one at first took for feathers were painted iron plates which as the animal opened and closed its wings to shake off the rain and blood formed an uncompromising perspective made up of smelly residues and the noises of spoons banged together by the white hands of an earthquake in the sordid baskets of a too unhealthy summer.

Marais

Le marais déroulant son lasso jusque là lové autour de son nombril le marais dégoisant les odeurs qui jusque là avaient tissé une épaule avec des aisselles Le marais défaisant le mauvais œil qui jusqu'à présent lui avait éclairé tant bien que mal le mauvais bouge au fond duquel il entretenait ses mauvaises raisons dans un bocal de sangsues luxueuses réservées aux sangs des plus illustres têtes couronnées

et me voilà installé par les soins obligeants de l'enlisement au fond du marais et fumant le tabac le plus rare qu'aucune alouette ait jamais fumé.

Miasme on m'avait dit que ce ne pouvait être que le règne du crépuscule.
Je te donne acte que l'on m'avait trompé. De l'autre côté de la vie, de la mort, montent des bulles. Elles éclatent à la surface avec un bruit d'ampoules électriques brisées. Ce sont les scaphandriers des victimes de la réclusion qui reviennent à la surface remiser leur tête de plomb et de verre leur tendresse.

Tout animal m'est agami-chien de garde.
Toute plante silphium-lascinatum parole aveugle du Nord et du Sud.
Pourtant alerte.
Ce sont les serpents.
L'un d'eux siffle le long de ma colonne vertébrale puis s'enroulant au plus bas de ma cage thoracique lance sa tête jusqu'à ma gorge spasmodique.
À la fin l'occlusion en est douce et j'entonne sous le sable

l'HYMNE AU SERPENT LOMBAIRE

Swamp

The swamp unrolling its lasso until then coiled around its navel the swamp
spouting odors that until then had woven a shoulder with armpits
The swamp unmaking the evil eye that up to the present had lit up more
or less well the miserable den in the depths of which it preserved its faulty
reasoning in a jar of luxurious leeches reserved for the blood of the most
illustrious crowned heads

and here I am settled via the most obliging quicksand at the bottom of the
swamp and smoking the rarest tobacco that any lark ever smoked.

Miasma they told me this could only be the reign of twilight. I hereby notify
you that I had been misled. From the other side of life, of death, bubbles are
rising. They burst on the surface with the sound of shattered light bulbs.
They are the divers of the victims of reclusion resurfacing to put away their
heads of lead and of glass their tenderness.

For me every animal is a trumpeter-watchdog.
Every plant a silphium blind word of the North and South.
But stay alert.
They are serpents.
One of them hisses along my spinal column then coiling at the base of my
thoracic cage it darts its head up to my spasmodic throat.
At the end the occlusion is sweet and beneath the sand I intone

the HYMN TO THE LUMBAR SERPENT

Couteaux Midi

Quand les Nègres font la Révolution ils commencent par arracher du Champ de Mars des arbres géants qu'ils lancent à la face du ciel comme des aboiements et qui couchent dans le plus chaud de l'air de purs courants d'oiseaux frais où ils tirent à blanc. Ils tirent à blanc? Oui ma foi parce que le blanc est la juste force controversée du noir qu'ils portent dans le cœur et qui ne cesse de conspirer dans les petits hexagones trop bien faits de leurs pores. Les coups de feu blancs plantent alors dans le ciel des belles de nuit qui ne sont pas sans rapport avec les cornettes des sœurs de Saint Joseph de Cluny qu'elles lessivent sous les espèces de midi dans la jubilation solaire du savon tropical. Midi? Oui, Midi qui disperse dans le ciel la ouate trop complaisante qui capitonne mes paroles et où mes cris se prennent. Midi? Oui Midi amande de la nuit et langue entre mes crocs de poivre. Midi? Oui Midi qui porte sur son dos de galeux et de vitrier toute la sensibilité qui compte de la haine et des ruines. Midi? pardieu Midi qui après s'être recueilli sur mes lèvres le temps d'un blasphème et aux limites cathédrales de l'oisiveté met sur toutes les lignes de toutes les mains les trains que la repentance gardait en réserve dans les coffres-forts du temps sévère. Midi? Oui Midi somptueux qui de ce monde m'absente.

Oh tyrannique et épanoui aux pieds d'écume orageuse et de vent et ton drapeau de guenilles claquant pour les heures gaspillées pour les jeux abandonnés pour les corbeaux présents pour les serpents futurs
filao filao
bien sûr que j'ai une gueule de mandragore
que son nom répond au mien
que son cri est le mien quand on m'a tiré du ventre phosphorescent de ma mère
bien sûr que mon crachat est mortel à certains
plus et mieux que l'ellébore varaire
bien sûr que j'ai plus de mépris qu'une graine de pissenlit
et plus de pudeur que le cirse des bois qui n'accomplit le fruit de sa copulation qu'entre ciel et terre

Mais filao filao pourquoi filao
en tout cas en ton nom filao je crache à ton visage santa maria
filao
filao
en tout cas je crache au visage des affameurs au visage des insulteurs au visage des paraschites et des éventreurs

Noon Knives

When the Blacks make Revolution they begin by uprooting from the Champ de Mars giant trees that they hurl like bayings into the face of the sky and that in the hottest of the air take aim at the pure streams of fresh birds at which they fire blanks. They fire blanks? Yes indeed because blankness is the disputed just force of the blackness that they bear in their hearts and that never ceases to conspire in the little too-well-made hexagons of their pores. The blank shots then plant in the sky ladies of the night that are not unrelated to the coifs of Saint Joseph de Cluny nuns which they launder under the bread and wine of noon amidst the solar jubilation of tropical soap. Noon? Yes, Noon dispersing in the sky the too complacent cotton wool that muffles my words and traps my screams. Noon? Yes Noon almond of the night and tongue between my pepper fangs. Noon? Yes Noon that bears on its scabby glazier's back all the sensitivity toward hatred and ruins that counts. Noon? by god Noon which after pausing on my lips just long enough for a curse and at the cathedral limits of idleness sets on all the lines of every hand the trains that repentance kept in reserve in the strong-boxes of severe time. Noon? Yes sumptuous Noon that absents me from this world.

Oh! tyrannical and radiant at the feet of stormy spume and wind and your tattered flag flapping for the wasted hours for the abandoned games for the present crows for the future serpents
filao filao
of course I have a mandrake mug
its name answers to mine
its scream is mine when I was ripped from my mother's phosphorescent womb
of course my spittle is deadly to some
more and better than white hellebore
of course I have more disdain than a dandelion seed
and greater modesty than wood thistle which realizes the fruit of its copulation only between sky and earth

But filao filao why filao
in any case in your name filao I spit in your face santa maria
filao
filao
in any case I spit in the face of the starvers in the face of the revilers in the face of the paraschites and the eviscerators

filao
filao
Mon monde est doux
doux comme l'hièble
doux comme le verre de catastrophe
doux comme le parfum d'une étoffe rouge sur la respiration bruyante d'une peau noire
doux comme la houppelande faite de plumes d'oiseau que la vengeance vêt après le crime
doux comme la démarche sûre et calomniée de l'aveugle
doux comme le salut des petites vagues surprises en jupes dans les chambres du mancenillier
doux comme un fleuve de mandibules et la paupière du perroquet
doux comme une pluie de cendre emperlée de petits feux
filao
oh
filao
debout dans mes blessures où mon sang bat contre les fûts du naufrage
des cadavres de chiens crevés d'où fusent des colibris
je tiens mon pacte
un jour pour nos pieds fraternels
un jour pour nos mains sans rancunes
un jour pour nos souffles sans méfiance
un jour pour nos faces sans vergogne

et les Nègres vont cherchant dans la poussière—à leur oreille à pleins poumons les pierres précieuses chantant—les échardes dont on fait le mica dont on fait les lunes et l'ardoise lamelleuse dont les sorciers font l'intime férocité des étoiles.

filao
filao
My world is sweet
sweet as the dwarf elder
sweet as the glass of catastrophe
sweet as the perfume of red fabric on the heavy breathing of a black skin
sweet as the greatcoat made of bird feathers that vengeance dons after
the crime
sweet as the sure and maligned gait of the blind man
sweet as the greeting of wavelets surprised in their petticoats in the chambers
of the manchineel
sweet as a river of mandibles and the eyelid of the parrot
sweet as a rain of ash empearled with tiny fires
filao
oh
filao
upright in my wounds where my blood beats against the shafts of shipwreck
of the cadavers of croaked dogs out of which hummingbirds are rocketing
I stick to my pact
a day for our fraternal feet
a day for our hands without rancor
a day for our breath without distrust
a day for our faces without shame

and the Blacks go searching in the dust—gems singing in their ears at
the top of their voices—for the splinters from which mica is made from
which moons are made and the fissile slate out of which sorcerers make the
intimate ferocity of the stars.

Idylle

Quand viendra le soir du monde que les réverbères seront de grandes filles
immobiles un nœud jaune aux cheveux et le doigt sur la bouche
quand la lumière dans la vitre coupera sa natte et fera frire ses œufs dans une
goutte de sang prise à la neige des blessés
que le vin lourd de midi lancera du grain aux étoiles de minuit
il y aura dans mon âme les légères corbeilles du brouillard qui seront
sommées de verser des bennes de lumière
la solitude ouvrira de minuscules fenêtres
sur la belle amitié radiophonique des nombres
et dans la reconversion du calendrier dans le feu de joie de la planche
à journées
le jour sera si pur qu'on y verra les jours

corbeau doux serviteur
comme moi rauque et voluptueux
butin de l'air épais et de l'espace bavard il y aura
une pompe d'auto décapitée sur le billot du temps à faire les loups
des ris d'enfants d'une récréation qu'on ne voit pas faisant penser aux
chaperons faisant penser aux dévorés faisant penser
aux prophètes que les hommes chassaient de leurs songes à coups de
pierre grise

corbeau
ton jour arrive sans but sur des pattes d'emprunt
comme un nègre domestique porteur de lait agile

corbeau
le dernier pendu tourne son œil légal dans le chaste zéro du repentir et
de l'absurde

corbeau suave chant de mandragore
comme moi vénéneux et tranquille
il y a encore à desceller les pierres bleues du château
et la géométrie sans peine du mensonge

corbeau
de ta noire signature honore la page blanche
échappée à la morte-saison des étreintes pucelles

Idyll

When the night of the world comes and the streetlamps become motionless
tall girls yellow bows in their hair and a finger to their lips
when the light in the pane cuts its pigtail and fries its eggs in a drop of blood
taken from the snow of the wounded
and the heavy wine of noon casts its seed to the midnight stars
there shall be airy baskets of fog in my soul that shall be summoned to pour
out buckets of light
solitude shall open miniscule windows
onto the beautiful radiophonic friendship of numbers
and in the reconversion of the calendar in the bonfire of the day planks
the day shall be so pure that days shall be visible in it

crow sweet servant
raucous and voluptuous like me
plunder of thick air and chatty space there shall be
a decapitated auto pump on the chopping block of time for making
wolf masks
the laughter of children at an unnoticed recess causing one to think of
chaperones causing one to think of the devoured causing one to think
of the prophets whom men hunted from their dreams with blows of
gray stone

crow
your day is coming without purpose on borrowed feet
like a house nigger bearing agile milk

crow
the last hanged man turns his legal eye in the chaste zero of repentance and
absurdity

suave crow song of the mandrake
venomous and tranquil like me
there are still to be loosened the blue stones of the castle
and the painless geometry of the lie

crow
with your black signature honor the white page
escaped from the dead season of virginal embraces

corbeau tête forte
debout derrière la trappe de ton cri
quand l'inventaire scrupuleux des mots de tous les jours commencera
car il sera temps de penser à des témoins moins velus que les astres
—sur quels sabots s'est enfuie ta présence? dira
surgi de la patience du trottoir et de la flamme du ruisseau
mon ange gardien
ses doigts terrestres près d'un bassin feuillu semant en vain
des mots à goût de pain et de piège

je ne répondrai rien
mais je le conduirai selon la méridienne
à l'épiphanie chaste d'une rosace de sang d'une gerbe de lumière du grand
effort brun d'une forge où se tord
la poussée noire du geste baignée de sable blanc

alors de celle qui réveille à leur vocation de boa constrictor
les routes étrangleuses du paysage qu'elles étaient chargées d'allaiter
à celle qui fait que les paons sacrés de ma vie incorruptible roucoulent
de remémoration
les bœufs rouges ramèneront la journée au tombeau où par écume une
chaleur de champagne pétillante de bourgeons et d'atolls
ouvrira des paumes lasses
dans l'air il y aura ouvriers du beau temps des ocelles et des cerfs de cristal
de grandes paroles vierges des alligators pieux dont nos oiseaux très sages
cureront les dents

sommeil noueur de racines
j'arrose tes guérets
capte la voix qui fait que les termites bâtissent haut
dans mon crâne leur pyramide funèbre tendue d'un vol de pigeons
multicolores

or toi oiseau frappé de la fronde des mirages
cognant ta tête au plafond du soleil
et des astres et des rêves et du néant
d'île en île eau claire que tu dédaignes
ô toi prisonnière de ta cire que vantent les parchemins
tu tomberas
froisseuse d'étoiles broyeuse d'herbes grand corps

strong-minded crow
upright behind the trapdoor of your cry
when the scrupulous inventory of everyday words begins
for it shall be time to think of witnesses less hairy than the stars
—in what clogs did your presence flee? my guardian angel
having arisen from the patience of the sidewalk and from the flame of
the gutter shall say
his terrestrial fingers near a leafy basin sowing in vain
words tasting of bread and of snare

I shall answer nothing
but I shall guide him along the meridian line
to the chaste epiphany of a blood rose window of a shower of light of the
great brown effort of a forge where writhes
the black thrust of a gesture bathed in white sand

then from she who awakens to their boa constrictor vocation
the strangler routes of the landscape that they were instructed to nurse
to she who makes the sacred peacocks of my incorruptible life warble with
recollection
the red oxen shall lead the day back to the tomb where afroth a champagne
warmth bubbling with buds and atolls
shall open tired palms
in the air there shall be fine weather workmen ocelli and crystal stags great
virginal words pious alligators whose teeth our very wise birds shall clean

sleep root-knotter
I water your fallow fields
capture the voice that makes termites build high
in my skull their funereal pyramid spanned by a flight of multicolored
pigeons

and you bird hit by the slingshot of mirages
beating your head on the ceiling of the sun
and of the stars and of dreams and of the void
from isle to isle the clear water that you disdain
oh you prisoner of your wax that parchments praise
you shall fall
crumpler of stars crusher of grasses great body

Mot de passe

Zélande je me mets au diapason
Zélande qui ne me donne jamais que le temps de ranger dans l'armoire de ma gorge tous les mots par lesquels j'avais pris les jours au piège d'un calendrier sans viscères
Zélande au fond du naufrage
Zélande avec autour un sol jonché de carapaces
Zélande à la rosace de zinnias
Zélande cil vibratile de l'innocence
Zélande dont les yeux sont une montre arrêtée sur une heure illisible
Zélande tempête mal lacée de noir sur le feu de la terre
Zélande mot de passe
Zélande hippobroma
Zélande concurrence d'antipode
Zélande ne m'interroge pas
Zélande je ne sais plus mon nom
au matin rouleur de la première force de la première épave de la dernière aurore
nos dents feront le bond d'une terre au haut d'un ciel de cannelle et de girofles
tu ouvriras tes paupières qui sont un éventail très beau
fait de plumes rougies de regarder mon sang battre
une saison triomphante des essences les plus rares
ce sera tes cheveux
ballant au vent puéril la nostalgie des longues canéfices

Password

Zealand I fall in with your mood
Zealand that only gives me time to stow in the armoire of my throat all the words with which I had caught the days in the trap of a gutless calendar
Zealand at the bottom of the shipwreck
Zealand with ground all around piled high with carapaces
Zealand of the zinnia rose window
Zealand vibratory eyelash of innocence
Zealand whose eyes are a watch stopped at an illegible hour
Zealand tempest badly laced with black across the fire of the earth
Zealand password
Zealand Star of Bethlehem
Zealand antipodal concurrence
Zealand do not interrogate me
Zealand I no longer know my name
in the morning leaf roller of the first force of the first wreckage of the final dawn
our teeth shall bound from an earth up to the height of a cinnamon and clove sky
you shall open your eyelids that are a very beautiful fan
made of feathers reddened from watching my blood throb
a triumphant season of the rarest essential oils
this shall be your hair
swinging the nostalgia of long cassia in the puerile wind

Tournure des choses

De vrai l'agiot des oiseaux du paradis ne fane plus la rose des vents et quand
j'ouvre la cage de mes paupières quand je dégante mes éperviers nichés et que
je les lance dans une détente de prunelles là où le pollen de la faim accomplit
sans bruit le haut miracle de la fécondation de la fleur stérile du désespoir
(écume de la parole jetée à l'étourdi parmi la flamme d'un silence
concrétion juste aperçue de mon sein gauche trop vivace
excroissance de la plus sauvage pratique de mes orteils
à ma volonté traînant les bribes du monde
à ma volonté ensablant des halètements de plus en plus faibles que je dispose
très bien en mondes sagement défunts)
justice au paysage! c'est lui le crieur encore lui
le chemin se sourit aux couchants
les pierres apprivoisent la mer démontée
les crabes qui sont les soleils des égouts révoltés contre l'ordre des voiries
sont suspendus au haut des palais anciens
mes mains se passent recroquevillées la cognée des présages
La ville? Néant de ville. La ville? Néant d'yeux néant de cauchemars néant
de souvenir néant d'indifférence

Turn of Events

Truly the stockjobbing of the birds of paradise no longer makes the rose of the winds fade and when I open the cage of my eyelids when I unglove my nested sparrowhawks and release them in a relaxing of eyeballs where the pollen of hunger noiselessly carries out the lofty miracle of fecundating the sterile flower of despair
(froth of the word tossed thoughtlessly amidst the flames of a silence
just concretion perceived by my excessively vivacious left breast
excrescence of the most uncivilized habits of my big toes
to my will dragging the scraps of the world
to my will silting up with more and more feeble gasps that I array quite nicely as wisely defunct worlds)
justice to the landscape! it is he the crier always he
the path smiles back at the sunsets
stones tame the raging sea
crabs that are the suns of sewers revolted against the order of the road system are suspended at the top of ancient palaces
my hands shriveled pass back and forth the blow of omens
The city? The nothingness of the city. The city? The nothingness of eyes the nothingness of nightmares the nothingness of memory the nothingness of indifference

Question préalable

Pour moi qu'on me serre la jambe
je rends une forêt de lianes
Qu'on me pende par les ongles
                        je pisse un chameau portant un pape et je
m'évanouis en une rangée de ficus qui très proprement enserrent l'intrus et
l'étranglent dans un beau balancement tropical
La faiblesse de beaucoup d'hommes est qu'ils ne savent devenir ni une pierre
ni un arbre
Pour moi je m'installe parfois des mèches soufrées entre mes doigts de boa
pour l'unique plaisir de m'enflammer en feuilles neuves de poinsettias tout
le soir
rouges et verts tremblant au vent
comme dans ma gorge notre aurore

Preliminary Question

As for me should they grab my leg
I vomit up a forest of lianas
Should they hang me by my fingernails
                        I piss a camel bearing a pope and vanish in a
row of fig trees that quite neatly encircle the intruder and strangle him in a
beautiful tropical balancing act
The weakness of many men is that they do not know how to become either a
stone or a tree
As for me I sometimes fit sulfurous wicks between my boa fingers for the sole
pleasure of bursting into a flame of new poinsettia leaves all evening long
reds and greens trembling in the wind
like our dawn in my throat

Tatouage des regards

Yeux accrochés à leur haut pédoncule hypertrophié yeux d'anacardier et pus
de tannin sur moi braqués comme un regard de mauvais fruit comme des
mouches d'abattoir comme une barbe de justicier
certes je suis du monde l'être le plus percé
chaque homme qui me rencontre s'adjugeant le droit de me planter un clou
au hasard de ma tête de mon cœur de mes mains de mes yeux

mais ma grande joie est de tromper les coups : férocité de mon intimité là où
ils pensaient trouver le vide – vide sable et friable bois de termite au lieu de
l'aubier qu'à volonté non saisonnière je me fabrique –

Penaude en est leur ancre
cependant que fait le gros dos et roucoule mon encre qui remonte encore
en sève à la surface me donner une couleur où commodément attendre et
surprendre (dans cette forêt où il faut être bête comme Christ et chou pour
être crucifié) l'imbécillité des coups de larrons des clous toujours à l'affût

Tattooing Gazes

Eyes attached to their tall hypertrophied peduncle cashew-tree and tannin pus eyes fixed on me like the gaze of bad fruit like slaughterhouse flies like a vigilante's beard
I am for sure the most pierced being in the world
each man who encounters me giving himself the right to drive a nail as chance directs at my head my heart my hands my eyes

but my greatest joy is to foil the blows: ferocity of my intimacy where they expected to find the void—void sand and crumbly termite wood in place of the sapwood that at my unseasonable pleasure I make for myself—

Contrite is their anchor
while lying low and cooing my ink still resurfaces as sap to give me a color in which conveniently to wait and to surprise (in this forest where one would have to be as stupid as Christ and cabbage to get crucified) the imbecility of robbers' blows of nails always lying in wait

Aux écluses du vide

Au premier plan et fuite longitudinale un ruisseau desséché sommeilleux rouleur de galets d'obsidiennes. Au fond une point quiète architecture de burgs démantelés de montagnes érodées sur le fantôme deviné desquels naissent serpents chariots œil de chat des constellations alarmantes. C'est un étrange gâteau de lucioles lancé contre la face grise du temps, un grand éboulis de tessons d'icones et de blasons de poux dans la barbe de Saturne. A droite très curieusement debout à la paroi squameuse de papillons crucifiés ailes ouvertes dans la gloire une gigantesque bouteille dont le goulot d'or très long boit dans les nuages une goutte de sang. Pour ma part je n'ai plus soif. Il m'est doux de penser le monde défait comme un vieux matelas à coprah comme un vieux collier vaudou comme le parfum du pécari abattu. Je n'ai plus soif. Toutes les têtes m'appartiennent. Il est doux d'être doux comme un agneau. Il est doux d'ouvrir les grandes vannes de la douceur :

> par le ciel ébranlé
> par les étoiles éclatées
> par le silence tutélaire
> de très loin d'outre moi je viens vers toi
> femme surgie d'un bel aubier
> et tes yeux blessures mal fermées
> sur ta pudeur d'être née

C'est moi qui chante d'une voix prise encore dans le balbutiement des éléments. Il est doux d'être un morceau de bois un bouchon une goutte d'eau dans les eaux torrentielles de la fin et du recommencement. Il est doux de s'assoupir au cœur brisé des choses. Je n'ai plus aucune espèce de soif. Mon épée faite d'un sourire de dents de requin devient terriblement inutile. Ma masse d'armes est très visiblement hors de saison et hors de jeu. La pluie tombe. C'est un croisement de gravats, c'est un écheveau de fer pour ciment armé, c'est un incroyable arrimage de l'invisible par des liens de toute qualité, c'est une ramure de syphilis, c'est le diagramme d'une saoulerie à l'eau-de-vie, c'est la représentation graphique d'une marée séismique, c'est un complot de cuscutes, c'est la tête du cauchemar fichée sur la pointe de lance d'une foule en délire de paix et de pain.
J'avance jusqu'à la région des lacs bleus. J'avance jusqu'à la région des solfatares

At the Locks of the Void

In the foreground and in longitudinal flight a dried-up brook drowsy roller of obsidian pebbles. In the background a decidedly not calm architecture of torn down burgs of eroded mountains on whose glimpsed phantom serpents chariots a cat's-eye and alarming constellations are born. It is a strange firefly cake hurled into the gray face of time, a vast scree of shards of ikons and of blazons of lice in the beard of Saturn. On the right very curiously standing against the squamous wall of crucified butterfly wings open in majesty a gigantic bottle whose very long golden neck drinks a drop of blood in the clouds. As for me I am no longer thirsty. It gives me pleasure to think of the world undone like an old copra mattress like an old Vodun necklace like the perfume of a felled peccary. I am no longer thirsty. All heads belong to me. It is sweet to be gentle as a lamb. It is sweet to open the great sluicegates of gentleness:

> through the staggered sky
> through the exploded stars
> through the tutelary silence
> from very far beyond myself I come toward you
> woman sprung from a beautiful laburnum
> and your eyes wounds barely closed
> on your modesty at being born

It is I who sing with a voice still caught up in the babbling of elements. It is sweet to be a piece of wood a cork a drop of water in the torrential waters of the end and of the new beginning. It is sweet to doze off in the shattered heart of things. I no longer have any sort of thirst. My sword made from a shark's-tooth smile is becoming terribly useless. My mace is very obviously out of season and out of play. Rain is falling. It is a crisscross of rubble, it is a skein of iron for reinforced concrete, it is an incredible stowage of the invisible by first-rate ties, it is a branchwork of syphilis, it is the diagram of a brandy bender, it is the graphic representation of a seismic floodtide, it is a conspiracy of dodders, it is the nightmare's head impaled on the lance point of a mob mad for peace and for bread.
I advance to the region of blue lakes. I advance to the region of sulphur springs

j'avance jusqu'à ma bouche cratériforme vers laquelle ai-je assez peiné?
Qu'ai-je à jeter ? Tout ma foi tout. Je suis tout nu. J'ai tout jeté. Ma généalogie.
Ma veuve. Mes compagnons. J'attends le bouillonnement, j'attends le
baptême de sperme. J'attends le coup d'aile du grand albatros séminal qui
doit faire de moi un homme nouveau. J'attends l'immense tape, le soufflet
vertigineux qui me sacrera chevalier d'un ordre plutonien. J'attends au plus
profond de mes pores la sacrée intrusion de la bénédiction.

Et subitement c'est le débouché des grands fleuves
c'est l'amitié des yeux de toucans
c'est l'érection au fulminate de montagnes vierges
je suis enceint avec mon désespoir dans mes bras
je suis enceint avec ma faim dans mes bras et mon dégoût dans la bouche.
je suis investi. L'Europe patrouille dans mes veines comme une meute de
filaires sur le coup de minuit. Dire que leurs philosophies ont essayé de leur
donner une morale. Cette race féroce ne l'aura pas supportée.

Europe éclat de fonte
Europe tunnel bas d'où suinte une rosée de sang
Europe carne Europe
Europe vieux chien Europe calèche à vers
Europe tatouage pelé Europe ton nom est un gloussement rauque et un choc
assourdi

je déplie mon mouchoir c'est un drapeau
j'ai mis ma belle peau
j'ai ajusté mes belles pattes onglées

Europe
je donne mon adhésion à tout ce qui poudroie le ciel de son insolent à tout
ce qui est loyal et fraternel à tout ce qui a le courage d'être éternellement
neuf à tout ce qui sait donner son cœur au feu à tout ce qui a la force de sortir
d'une sève inépuisable à tout ce qui est calme et sûr
à tout ce qui n'est pas toi
Europe
nom considérable de l'étron

I advance to my crateriform mouth toward which have I struggled enough?
What have I to discard? Everything by god everything. I am stark naked.
I have discarded everything. My genealogy. My widow. My companions. I
await the boiling, I await the baptism of sperm. I await the wingbeat of the
great seminal albatross supposed to make a new man of me. I await the
immense tap, the vertiginous slap that shall consecrate me as a knight of a
plutonian order. I await in the depths of my pores the sacred intrusion of the
benediction.

And suddenly it is the outpouring of great rivers
it is the friendship of toucans' eyes
it is the fulminating erection of virgin mountains
I am pregnant with my despair in my arms
I am pregnant with my hunger in my arms and my disgust in my mouth.
I am invested. Europe patrols my veins like a pack of filariae at the stroke of
midnight. To think that their philosophies tried to provide them with morals.
That ferocious race won't have put up with it.

Europe pig iron fragment
Europe low tunnel oozing a bloody dew
Europe old bag Europe
Europe old dog Europe worm-drawn coach
Europe peeling tattoo Europe your name is a raucous clucking and a muffled
shock

I unfold my handkerchief it is a flag
I have donned my beautiful skin
I have adjusted my beautiful clawed paws

Europe
I hereby join all that powders the sky with its insolence all that is loyal and
fraternal all that has the courage to be eternally new all that knows how
to yield its heart to the fire all that has the strength to emerge from an
inexhaustible sap all that is calm and certain
all that is not you
Europe
eminent name of the turd

Déshérence

Dès que je presse le petit déclic que j'ai sous la langue en un endroit qui échappe à toute détection à tout bombardement microscopique à toute divination de sourcier à toute prospection de savant sous sa triple épaisseur de faux cils de siècles d'insultes de strates de madrépores de ce qu'il me faut appeler ma caverne à niagara dans un éclat de cancrelats dans une crispation de cobra une langue comme un sujet d'étonnement fait le bond d'une machine à cracher une gueule de malédictions une remontée des égouts de l'enfer une éjaculation prémonitoire un jaillissement urinaire une émission méphitique un rythme de soufre alimentant une ininterruption d'interjections — et alors voilà poussant entre les pavés les furieux eucalyptus bleus du pétrole qui laissent bien loin derrière eux la splendeur des véroniques les crânes à même le délire de la poussière comme la prune jaboticaba et alors voilà commencé dans un gros bourdonnement de frelon la vraie guerre de dévolution où tous les moyens sont bons voilà que montent les pigeons voyageurs de l'incendie voilà le crépitement des postes secrets et les épaisses touffes de fumée noire qui ressemblent à des végétations vaginales lancées en l'air par le coup de reins du rut. Je compte. À travers la rue une armillaire couleur de miel c'est couchée nainement sur le flanc une église déracinée et réduite par la catastrophe à ses vraies proportions de pissotière. Je passe sur des ponts écroulés. Je passe sous des arceaux nouveaux. Œil luge au bas d'une joue parmi les bois et les cuivres bien astiqués une maison à flanc d'abîme avec en coupe la virginité violée de la jeune fille de la maison les corps et biens du père et de la mère perdus qui croyaient à la dignité de l'homme et dans le fond d'un bas de laine les testicules percés d'une aiguille à tricoter d'un chômeur des pays lointains. Je porte la main à mon front c'est une couvée de moussons. Je porte la main à ma queue. Elle s'est évanouie dans une fumée de feuilles. Toute la lumière désertrice du ciel s'est réfugiée dans les barres chauffées à rouge à blanc à jaune des serpents attentifs au dépérissement de ce paysage méprisé par le pissat des chiens.
À quoi bon ?
Les planètes sont des oiseaux très fertiles qui à tout moment déclosent majestueusement leurs silos à guano
la terre sur sa broche vomit alternativement la graisse de chacune de ses faces

Forfeiture

As soon as I press the little pawl that I have under my tongue at a spot that escapes all detection all microscopic bombardment all dowser divination all scholarly prospecting beneath its triple thickness of false eyelashes of centuries of insults of strata of madrepores of what I must call my niagara cavern in a burst of cockroaches in a cobra twitch a tongue like a cause for astonishment makes the leap of a machine for spitting a mouthful of curses a rising of the sewers of hell a premonitory ejaculation a urinary spurt a foul emission a sulfuric rhythm feeding an uninterruption of interjections—and then right there pushing between the paving stones the furious blue petroleum eucalypti that leave far behind them the splendor of veronicas, skulls right in the delirium of dust like the jaboticaba plum and then right there started up like the loud buzzing of a hornet the true war of devolution in which all means are justified right there the passenger pigeons of the conflagration right there the crackling of secret transmitters and the thick tufts of black smoke that resemble the vaginal vegetation thrust into the air by rutting loins. I count. Obstructing the street a honey-colored armillaria lying dwarflike on its side a church uprooted and reduced by catastrophe to its true proportions of a public urinal. I cross over collapsed bridges. I cross under new arches. Toboggan eye at the bottom of a cheek amidst woodwinds and well-polished brasses a house abutting an abyss with in cut-away view the violated virginity of the daughter of the house the lost goods and chattels of the father and the mother who believed in the dignity of mankind and in the bottom of a wool stocking the testicles pierced by a knitting needle of an unemployed workman from distant lands.
I place my hand on my forehead it's a hatching of monsoons. I place my hand on my dick. It fainted in leaf smoke. All the deserter light of the sky has taken refuge in the red white and yellow heated bars of snakes attentive to the wasting away of this landscape sneered at by dog piss.
For what?
The planets are very fertile birds that constantly and majestically disclose their guano silos
the earth on its spit alternatively vomits grease from each of its facets

des poignées de poissons accrochent leurs feux de secours aux pilastres des astres dont le vieux glissement s'effrite dans la nuit en une épaisse saveur très amère de coca.

À qui d'entre vous n'est-il jamais arrivé de frapper une terre à cause de la malice de ses habitants ? Aujourd'hui je suis debout et dans la seule blancheur que les hommes ne m'ont jamais connue.

fistfuls of fish hook their emergency lights to the pilasters of stars whose ancient slippage crumbles away during the night in a thick very bitter flavor of coca.

Who among you has never happened to strike an earth because of its inhabitants' malice? Today I am standing and in the sole whiteness that men have never recognized in me.

À la nuit

C'est sans doute cette femme dont l'astrologue et la géomancie m'avaient
révélé la date et le lieu d'apparition
et dont j'aurai mal tenu compte
et qui fait contre-jour de la voix des mares mal prises aux nasses des scirpes
contre-jour des hauts fourneaux du suicide
contre-jour des bernicles qui accrochent aux roches un gros bouquet de
jonquilles pour dire que le printemps est là
quand le vent a mis une pelure de papier sur un vieux peigne
quand le vent le plus vieux des nègres vieux souffle dedans une musique
où les jambes des jolies fables sortent d'une bruyère faite de la laine aimable
de loups écumeurs d'une litanie de chiens

ou bien sacrée mer d'Iroise debout et qui attend de moi une parole qui
signifie *pas de crainte* et qui assurément ne viendra pas
c'est la Grâce ou la Disgrâce
c'est le petit trot du cœur dans la maladie horlogère dite de Basedow

c'est la Grâce c'est la Disgrâce
la Disgrâce ou la Hargne
la Hargne aux dents de sourd qui dispose son filet de dents ébréchées
semblables à un sous-bois au tournant du mystère des oreillettes

la Hargne qui martèle ses mots et rafle toutes les mises
la Hargne faite à l'image de Dieu qui crée à petits coups de couteau qui
mijotent dans l'instruction d'une gaine prise dans la gayac de la rouille
où pas plus
que
        tu ne lèves ton visage
        le petit filet de sang de première communion que
        je ne répands pas
        pas plus
que ne se lève mon visage de pétrole à cacher ses liaisons les plus innocentes
pas plus que l'on n'en peut attendre de la rancune de nos visages mal fermés
et d'où coule plus sûr le site
que le sourire où nous mêlons de veine et d'artère nos deux sangs à la parole
inégale

To the Night

It was no doubt that woman whose date and place of apparition the
astrologer and the geomancy had revealed to me
and whom I haven't properly taken into account
and who appears backlit against the swamp voices wrongly caught in the
eel-pots of the bulrushes
backlit against the blast furnaces of suicide
backlit against the limpets that attach a huge bouquet of jonquils to the rocks
to say spring is here
when the wind has placed onion-skin paper on an old comb
when the oldest wind of the old niggers blows a tune on it
where the legs of pretty fables emerge from heather made of the loveable
wool of wolves plunderers of a litany of dogs

or again the sacred Iroise sea vertical and waiting for a word from me that
means *no fear* and that assuredly shall not come
it is Grace or Disgrace
it is the slow trot of the heart in the horological malady called Basedow's
disease

it is Grace it is Disgrace
Disgrace or Aggression
Aggression whose deaf man teeth display their net of broken teeth like an
undergrowth at the bend of the mystery of auricles

Aggression that hammers in its words and scoops up all the bets
Aggression made in the image of God who creates with little knife jabs who
simmers in the instruction of a sheath caught up in the guaiacum of rust
where no more
than
        you raise your face
        the little stream of first communion blood that I do not shed
        no more
than my petroleum face is raised to hide its most innocent liaisons
no more than one can expect from the rancor of our poorly closed faces from
whence flows most surely the site
than the smile in which we blend of vein and artery our two bloods of
unequal speech

Quelconque

Quelconque le gâteau de la nuit décoré de petites bougies faites de lucioles
quelconque une rangée de palmiers à éventer mes pensées les mieux tues
quelconque le plat du ciel servi par des mages en drap de piment rouge
quelconque la jeune main verte du poinsettia se crispant hors de ses gants
à massacre
Espoir Espoir
lorsque la vague déroule son paquet de lianes de toute odeur et toutes les
lance au cou de chevaux bigles
lorsque l'anse développe sa crinière de sel godronnée au plus rare amidon
d'algues et de poissons
que la gueule vomissante des victimes crache sa bouteille d'essence pas mal
conservée sous la masse ultra-mobile des montagnes montées sur feu central
tandis que l'alchimiste de l'aube fait rouler ses billes de diamant sur la main
de vaste feuille qu'agite l'alambic du tarot au milieu de sa cour d'arums pieux
Espoir quand les enfants découpés en tranches les hommes tués à coups de
pioche les femmes découpées en seins se nouent en grenades incendiaires
Espoir plane Grand Duc
Espoir troupeau d'éléphants lance une forêt tardive à l'engrais des étoiles
danse Espoir et piétine et crie parmi les attentions charmantes des remoras
et le beuglement neuf qu'émet le caïman à l'imminence d'un tremblement
de terre

blessure admirable je perds mon sang je perds mon souffle je perds ma tête et
la retrouve au débouché de la digestion des grands boas chère tête je te revêts
des innombrables pinnules qui me servent à briser la violence de la pluie
chère tête je te reperds je perds la mémoire je ne la retrouve pas je m'en fous
car au point de mes mutilations d'autres membres me naissent

que les graines volantes strient l'air de leurs hélices
que les lianes balafrent le vide de grands coups de rasoir
que les racines s'envoient dans ma gorge veloutée de grands coups de rhum
macéré de fourmis vénéneuses
Espoir je suis un petit tourbillon je pivote sur un moi-même avaleur de mares
sur un moi-même avaliseur de désastres et j'ouvre de ma gueule les écluses
de la reconstruction
Espoir aurore et couchant abattus c'est un bilan de cloches vaincues dans une
âpre poussière de sang
et par le serment d'une langue de chien

Commonplace

Commonplace the night cake decorated with little candles made of fireflies
commonplace a row of palm trees for exposing my thoughts best silenced
commonplace the plate of sky served by magi in red pepper raiment
commonplace the poinsettia's young green hand clenched outside its massacre gloves
Hope Hope
when the wave unrolls its bundle of lianas of every scent and casts all of them at the necks of cross-eyed horses
when the cove displays its salty mane gadrooned with the rarest starch of seaweed and fish
may the vomiting mugs of victims spit their bottles of essential oils not so badly preserved under the ultra-mobile mass of mountains risen over the central fire while the alchemist of dawn rolls his diamond beads across the vast leaf hand shaken by the tarot alembic in the midst of its pious arum court
Hope when the children cut up in pieces the men killed by pickaxe blows the women cut up into breasts are knotted into incendiary grenades
Hope soar Great Horned Owl
Hope herd of elephants hurl a tardy forest to the fertilizer of the stars
dance Hope and trample and scream among the remoras' charming attention and the raw bellowing the caiman emits at the onset of an earthquake

admirable wound I lose my blood I lose my breath I lose my head and find it again at the outfall of the digestion of great boa constrictors dear head I dress you with the innumerable pinnules that allow me to break the violence of the rain dear head I lose you again I lose my memory I don't recover it don't give a damn since right where my mutilations are other limbs grow back

may flying seeds striate the air with their propellers
may lianas gash the void with great razor slashes
may roots wash down my velvety throat huge shots of rum macerated with poisonous ants
Hope I am a little whirlwind I pivot on a myself swallower of ponds on a myself endorser of disasters and I open the floodgates of reconstruction with my mug
Hope sunrise and sunset struck down it is a balance sheet of conquered bells in a bitter bloody dust
and by the oath of a dog's tongue

et par le paradis épelé par la charogne dans l'éclaircie au petit bonheur du chiendent
et pourquoi pas voici monter ma tête premier pas du chaos
et mes bras chargés de dentelles tissées sur le métier majestueux de la crue et ma poitrine piétinée d'un pré de sensitives
c'est l'heure où jeter un delta desséché à travers mon visage et sur l'immense décombre je dessine d'impatience ma bouche toute nouvelle
Espoir l'étincellement d'un verglas aux temps forts de méduses
Espoir la flottaison juste de tes attitudes luttant avec le fourvoiement du mécanisme terrestre
Espoir j'élabore à mon flanc une haie si vive qu'une main des plis de mon cou fait jaillir cent calaos
Espoir il n'est pas trop tard je donne tout
à l'inoubliable claquement d'os de la malaria à la remarquable précision d'incision de la chauve-souris vampire je lègue ce qui me reste mes dix orteils mes dents adultes

et vous lanternes d'ibis enlevez au pas de vos épaules ma houppelande de vieux crachat et ma chemise de pistolet

Espoir Espoir
grande araigne au baiser de mes longs bras mécaniciens

and by the spelled-out paradise by the carrion in the haphazard couch-grass glade
and why not go on excite me the first step of chaos
and my arms filled with lace woven on the majestic loom of the flood and my chest trampled by a meadow of mimosas
it is the hour for throwing a desiccated delta across my face and on the immense wreckage I sketch impatiently my utterly new mouth
Hope the spark of a glare of ice in the downbeat of jellyfish
Hope the just flotsam of your attitudes struggling with the astray terrestrial mechanism
Hope I design on my side a hedge so alive that one hand can from the folds of my neck make a hundred hornbills burst forth
Hope it is not too late I give everything
to the unforgettable cracking of malarial bones to the remarkable precision of the incision of the vampire bat I bequeath what I have left my ten toes my adult teeth

and you ibis lanterns carry off at the pace of your shoulders my mantle of old spit and my pistol shirt

Hope Hope
great arain in the kiss of my long mechanic arms

Ode à la Guinée

Et par le soleil installant sous ma peau une usine de force et d'aigles
et par le vent sur ma force de dent de sel compliquant ses passes les
mieux sues
et par le noir le long de mes muscles en douces insolences de sèves montant
et par la femme couchée comme une montagne descellée et sucée par les
lianes
et par la femme au cadastre mal connu où le jour et la nuit jouent à la mourre
des eaux de source et des métaux rares
et par le feu de la femme où je cherche le chemin des fougères et du
Fouta-Djallon
et par la femme fermée sur la nostalgie s'ouvrant
donc
peuples de mares
couvrez de mares les champs de vos ciels longs
aux bas taillis jetez vos prophètes
et leurs oiseaux mettez à la nourrice des rouges mourons
certes et à l'heure où au cadran des dompteurs
le soleil coupe le sein des otaries
ô amazones
par le vagissement de l'arc
par la gloire de mes nuits
par mes lombes plus que jamais giclants
par la brune odeur d'un matin remué à mes narines
du fond d'un délirium sans tremblement
        JE TE SALUE
Guinée dont les pluies fracassent du haut grumeleux
des volcans un sacrifice de vaches pour mille faims
et soifs d'enfants dénaturés
Guinée bois et plante belle folle et grimpante
pierre frottée dont jamais ne jaillit une lumière femelle
Guinée à vrilles si
tous les gins plus chaudement bus que le sang ourdi des golfes j'avais une
sébile à soutirer comme des arbres le sang fructueux de tes femmes
par mes pieds salut Guinée
forêt
salut allée ouverte de tous côtés
Guinée oh cris

Ode to Guinea

And by the sun installing under my skin a factory of power and eagles
and by the wind upon my salt-tooth power complicating its best-known
passings
and by the black along my muscles in sweet sap effronteries rising
and by the woman supine like a mountain unsealed and sucked by lianas
and by the woman with the little-known cadastre where day and night play
mora for spring water and precious metals
and by the fire of the woman in whom I seek the road of ferns and
Fouta Jallon
and by the closed woman opening upon nostalgia
therefore
peoples of the ponds
cover with ponds the fields of your long skies
into the low copse cast your prophets
and put their birds out to the wet nurse of the reds surely
let us die and at the hour when on the dial of the subduers
the sun slashes the eared seal's breast
oh amazons
by the wailing of the bow
by the glory of my nights
by my loins spurting more than ever
by the brown odor of a morning agitated in my nostrils
from the depth of a delirium without trembling
           I HAIL YOU
Guinea whose rains from the curdled summits of volcanoes
shatter a cattle sacrifice for a thousand hungers
and thirsts of unnatural children
Guinea wood and plant beautiful wild and climbing
rubbed stone from which never sparks a female light
Guinea with tendrils if
all the gin drunk hotter than the plaited blood of the gulfs I had a begging
bowl to decant as from the trees the fruitful blood of your women
by my feet hail Guinea
forest
hail the alley open on all sides
Guinea oh! the cries

comme le corps des évadés tombant vierges dans le camp posthume de la
forêt
Guinée oh cris
comme des aiguilles de sel gemme
Guinée oh cris
alizé ou mousson
Guinée de ton cri de ta main de ta patience
il nous reste toujours des terres arbitraires
et quand tué vers Ophir ils m'auront jamais muet
de mes dents de ma peau que l'on fasse
un fétiche féroce gardien du mauvais œil

comme m'ébranle me frappe et me dévore ton solstice
en chacun de tes pas Guinée
muette au demeurant d'une profondeur astrale de méduses

like the bodies of escapees falling virginal into the posthumous camp of the forest
Guinea oh! the cries
like rock salt needles
Guinea oh! the cries
trade wind or monsoon
Guinea of your cry of your hand of your patience
there remain for us always some arbitrary lands
and when killed near Ophir leaving me mute forever
out of my teeth out of my skin let there be made
a ferocious fetish guardian of the evil eye

as your solstice shakes me strikes me and devours me
with each step you take Guinea
mute after all from an astral depth of medusas

Cheval
À Pierre Loeb

Mon cheval bute contre des crânes joués à la marelle de la rouille
mon cheval se cabre dans un orage de nuages qui sont des putréfactions de chairs à naufrage
mon cheval hennit dans la petite pluie de roses et de sentiments que fait mon sang dans le décor des fêtes foraines
mon cheval bute aux buissons de cactus qui sont les nœuds de vipère de mes tourments
mon cheval bute hennit et bute vers le rideau de sang de mon sang tiré sur tous les ruffians qui jouent aux dés mon sang
mon cheval bute devant l'impossible flamme de la barre que hurlent les vésicules de mon sang
mon cheval se cabre devant un grand pilier d'hyacinthe toute pure qui s'élève jusqu'à la gloire du seigneur et descend jusqu'au fond de la merde de mon sang
mon cheval se cabre devant une lampe de béryl faite des vers luisants que colporte mon sang
je vis aussi un grand cheval de paix ardente qui s'élançait en piaffant d'une saison de pluies de mollusques d'une colère de poils d'une harangue de pyramides d'une camisole de vieux bouchons d'une confusion de crachats de champignons
grand cheval mon sang à répandre sur les places publiques
mon sang où de temps en temps une femme en perfection de soleil lance toutes ses tiges tubéreuses et disparaît dans une tornade née de l'autre côté du monde
mon sang pour pied fraîchement repeint de gibet
mon sang qu'aucune canonisation n'a jamais souillé
mon sang vin de vomissure d'ivrogne
mon sang qu'aucun juge payé n'a jamais entendu
je te le donne grand cheval
je te donne mes oreilles pour en faire des naseaux sachant frémir
mes cheveux pour en faire une crinière des mieux sauvages
ma langue pour en faire des sabots de mustang
je te les donne
grand cheval

Horse
For Pierre Loeb

My horse stumbles over skulls hopscotched in rust
my horse rears in a storm of clouds that are putrefactions of shipwrecked flesh
my horse neighs in the fine rain of roses and sentiments that my blood creates in the scenery of the street fairs
my horse stumbles over the clumps of cacti that are the entangled vipers of my torments
my horse stumbles neighs and stumbles toward the curtain of blood of my blood pulled down on all the pimps shooting craps for my blood
my horse stumbles before the impossible flame of the barrier howled at by the vesicles of my blood
my horse rears before a great pillar of hyacinth perfectly pure that rises to the glory of the lord and descends to the depths of the shit of my blood
my horse rears before a beryl lamp made from fireflies peddled by my blood
I saw too a great horse of ardent peace that dashed forward pawing the ground from a season of rains of mollusks of an anger of hairs of a harangue of pyramids of a camisole of old corks of a confusion of mushroom spittle
great horse my blood to be spilled in public squares
my blood in which from time to time a woman in solar perfection shoots out all her tuberous stems and vanishes in a tornado born on the far side of the world
my blood for a foot freshly repainted as a gibbet
my blood that no canonization has ever soiled
my blood the wine of a drunkard's vomit
my blood that no paid-off judge has ever heard
I give it to you great horse
I give you my ears to be made into nostrils capable of quivering
my hair to be made into a mane as wild as they come
my tongue to be made into mustang hooves
I give them to you
great horse

pour que tu abordes à l'extrême limite de la fraternité
les hommes d'ailleurs et de demain
avec sur le dos un enfant aux lèvres à peine remuées du sillon
qui pour toi
désarmera
la mie chlorophyllienne des vastes corbeaux de l'avenir.

so that you may approach the extreme limit of brotherhood
the men of elsewhere and of tomorrow
on your back a child of the furrow with barely moving lips
who for you
shall disarm
the chlorophyllian crumb of the vast crows of the future.

Demeure antipode

Creuset où naît le monde cheveu humus de la première terre
cheveu première pierre du souci
lorsque la pluie sera le fil dont brin par brin le monde se défait
lorsque le soleil sera une araignée où nous perdre un par un
lorsque la mer sera un poulpe pour nous cracher nos espoirs à la face
lorsque la lune se délovera et nous déroulera son long corps de serpent
lorsque le volcan secouera son corps plissé de pachyderme
lorsque le vent ne soufflera plus parce qu'on aura oublié de frapper sur les
pierres à vent
lorsque les pierres cesseront de parler pour avoir trop prêché dans le désert
(emmêlement mes veines toute la forêt depuis ses basses branches
emmêlement mes veines l'eau tout entière et le régime des feux fidèles
emmêlement qui du fond me jettera des nénuphars à la face et mon sang de
rachat et mes épaules mieux coulantes que tous les nœuds
emmêlement
goutte d'eau dans l'alambic précieux des nappes aquifères qui se mettront à
la fenêtre et crieront qu'il fait beau dans l'espéranto mal entendu des volutes
striées de nos crachats les plus amers)
goutte de feu dans la gorge sans hasard du vent
luciole et eau je me construirai moi-même en petites gouttes d'eau de feu trop
belles pour un autre architecte

demeure faite d'eau entrevue au réveil
demeure faite de parfums froissés
demeure faite de sommeils lamés
demeure faite des jabots tendus des lézards engourdis
la force m'aligne sur le méridien sans ombre

pythons équipages de catastrophes frères dénaturés de ma longitude
les routes se haussent à la hauteur des gnomides à l'œil vert se coupent de
prières nous couchant en joue sur la passerelle du ciel déréglé de la boussole

Antipodal Dwelling

Crucible in which is born the world hair humus of the first earth
hair first worry stone
when the rain shall be the thread with which bit by bit the world undoes itself
when the sun shall be a spider in which to lose ourselves one by one
when the sea shall be an octopus to spit our hopes at us in our faces
when the moon shall uncoil and shall unroll for us its long serpent body
when the volcano shall shake its wrinkled pachyderm body
when the wind shall no longer blow because we have forgotten to strike the wind stones
when the stones shall cease to speak for having preached too much in the desert
(entangling my veins an entire forest down to its lowest branches
entangling my veins completely the water and the regime of faithful fires
entangling that from the bottom shall dash waterlilies in my face and my blood of redemption and my shoulders slipping better than any knots entangling
a drop of water in the precious alembic of water tables that shall go to the window and cry out in Esperanto that the weather is fine poorly understood by the volutes scored by our bitterest spit)
a drop of fire in the throat without risk of wind
firefly and water I shall assemble myself in little drops of water of fire too beautiful for any other architect

dwelling made of water glimpsed upon waking
dwelling made of rumpled perfumes
dwelling made of spangled sleep
dwelling made of swelled chests stretched out of benumbed lizards
strength lines me up on the shadowless meridian

pythons crews of catastrophes unnatural brothers of my longitude
roads raise themselves to the height of green-eyed female gnomes intersected with prayers taking aim at us on the footbridge of the malfunctioning compass sky

demeure faite d'une imposition de paumes de mains
demeure faite d'yeux rouges de guépard
demeure faite d'une pluie de coquilles de sable

les coups de revolver me font cette fois une auréole trop vaste pour ma tête
qui arrive par portage en pièces détachées

dwelling made of a laying-on of palms of hands
dwelling made of red cheetah eyes
dwelling made of a rain of shells of sand

the revolver shots give me a halo too vast this time for my head which arrives via portage in spare parts

Soleil et eau

Mon eau n'écoute pas
mon eau chante comme un secret
Mon eau ne chante pas
mon eau exulte comme un secret
Mon eau travaille
et à travers tout roseau exulte
jusqu'au lait du rire
Mon eau est un petit enfant
mon eau est un sourd
mon eau est un géant qui te tient sur la poitrine un lion
O vin
ô rampeur d'eau soulagé jusqu'à toi jusqu'aux arbres
vaste immense
par le basilic de ton regard complice et somptueux

Sun and Water

My water won't listen
my water sings like a secret
My water doesn't sing
my water rejoices like a secret
My water works
and through every reed rejoices
unto the very milk of laughter
My water is a little child
my water is a deaf man
my water is a giant holding a lion against your chest
Oh wine
oh water creeper released unto you unto the trees
vast immense
by the basilisk of your complicitous and sumptuous gaze

D'une métamorphose

Dernier râle du mourant dans le dernier rayon du soleil
jamblique oblique
et
pope
À Changhaï ramassons les enfants offerts sur la pelle de leur squelette aux
bêtes féroces de la famine
mais l'hivernage mais tes cheveux de glu qui collent tes yeux et les pestilences
touffues qui montent de tes cuisses plus vierges que les forêts nous n'en
saurions que faire aux razzias du déclic de pans d'Insulinde
quand Inde et Gange (tsumami tsumami) jouent à cache-cache avec
le Krakatoa
Ami tsumami et toi Gange grange-aux-tubercules pour récoltes submarines
ma sauvage
ma grandiose
d'une métamorphose sortons par un petit temps de pluie dans une rue côté
impair de Chicago
avec cervelle toute neuve d'abattoir et main toute fraîche de mercure
et qu'importe que la visibilité se brouille
nos poings se serrent sur la confiance hygiénique
l'aube le soir
la fusion est plus intense et intime qu'à tout moment du crépuscule
à cette heure précisément incroyablement forte
où dans le lit et à hauteur du Tropique du Cancer
s'allument et se perpétuent dans le vin des entailles des flux et de
l'enivrement les formidables amours du calmar et du cachalot

infirmes les hommes que nous rencontrons
car les bossus sont le meilleur antidote que l'on connaisse contre les curés

From a Metamorphosis

Last rattle of the dying man in the final ray of the sun
oblique jamblique
and
Eastern Orthodox priest
In Shanghai let us scoop up the children offered on the shovels of their
skeletons to the ferocious beasts of famine
but the rainy season but your birdlime hair that glues your eyes and the bushy
pestilences that rise from your thighs more virginal than forests we shall not
know what to do about the razzias of the trigger parts of the East Indies
when India and the Ganges (tsunami tsunami) play hide-and-seek with
Krakatoa
Friend tsunami and you Ganges tuber-barn for underseas crops
my wild
my grandiose
from a metamorphosis let us go out under a light rain onto the odd-
numbered side of a Chicago street
with a brand-new slaughterhouse brain and a thoroughly fresh mercurial
hand
and so what if the visibility is blurry
our fists are clenched on a hygienic confidence
the daybreak the evening
the fusion is most intense and intimate that at every crepuscular moment
at that hour precisely incredibly strong
when in bed and at the latitude of the Tropic of Cancer
the tremendous loves of the squid and the sperm whale spark and perpetuate
themselves in the wine of the gashes of flux and inebriation

crippled the men that we encounter
for hunchbacks are the best antidote we know of to priests

Marche des perturbations

Une robuste foudre en menace sur
le front le plus intouchable du monde
En toi toute la lumière veuve
des crépuscules des cités poignardées
par les oiseaux alentour
Et prends garde au corbeau qui ne vole pas c'est ma tête
qui s'est extraite du poteau mitan de mes épaules
en poussant un vieux cri arracheur d'entrailles et d'abreuvoirs

Ornières ornières lait doux brasier de flambes et d'euphorbes

March of Perturbations

A robust thunderbolt threatening over
the most untouchable brow in the world
In you all the light widow
of dusks of cities stabbed
by the region's birds
And watch out for the crow that does not fly it is my head
that extracted itself from the center post of my shoulders
uttering an ancient shriek ripper of entrails and watering troughs

Ruts ruts sweet milk brazier of flames and euphorbia

Barbare

C'est le mot qui me soutient
et frappe sur ma carcasse de cuivre jaune
où la lune dévore dans la soupente de la rouille
les os barbares
des lâches bêtes rôdeuses du mensonge

Barbare
du langage sommaire
et nos faces belles comme le vrai pouvoir opératoire
de la négation

Barbare
des morts qui circulent dans les veines de la terre
et viennent se briser parfois la tête contre les murs de nos oreilles
et les cris de révolte jamais entendus
qui tournent à mesure et à timbres de musique

Barbare
l'article unique
barbare le tapaya
barbare l'amphisbène blanche
barbare moi le serpent cracheur
qui de mes putréfiantes chairs me réveille
soudain gekko volant
soudain gekko frangé
et me colle si bien aux lieux mêmes de la force
qu'il vous faudra pour m'oublier
jeter aux chiens la chair velue de vos poitrines

Barbarity

This is the word that sustains me
and strikes against my brass carcass
where in the rust garret the moon devours
the barbarous bones
of cowardly prowling beasts of the lie

Barbarity
of rudimentary language
and our faces beautiful as the true operative power
of negation

Barbarity
of the dead circulating in the veins of the earth
who at times come to smash their heads against the walls of our ears
and the screams of revolt never heard
that turn in tune and musical tone

Barbarity
the singular article
barbarity the horned lizard
barbarity the white amphisbaena
barbarity I the spitting cobra
from my putrifying flesh awakening
suddenly a flying gecko
suddenly a fringed gecko
and I adhere so well to the very loci of strength
that to forget me you'll have to
throw the hairy flesh of your chests to the dogs

Cercle non vicieux

Penser est trop bruyant
a trop de mains pousse trop de hannetons
Du reste je ne me suis jamais trompé
les hommes ne m'ont jamais déçu ils ont des regards qui les débordent
La nature n'est pas compliquée
Toutes mes suppositions sont justes
Toutes mes implications fructueuses
Aucun cercle n'est vicieux
Creux
Il n'y a que mes genoux de noueux et qui s'enfonceront pierreux dans
le travail
des autres et leur sommeil

Non-Vicious Circle

Thinking is too noisy
has too many hands grows too many cockchafers
Moreover I have never been wrong
men have never disappointed me they have gazes that transcend them
Nature is not complicated
All my assumptions are correct
All my implications fruitful
No circle is ever vicious
Hollow
It is just my knees that are knotty and that shall sink stonelike into the labor of others and their sleep

Autre horizon

Nuit stigmate fourchu
nuit buisson télégraphique planté dans l'océan
pour minutieuses amours de cétacés
nuit fermée
pourrissoir splendide
où de toutes ses forces de tous ses fauves se ramasse
le muscle violet de l'aconit napel d'un autre soleil

Different Horizon

Night forked stigmata
night telegraphic bush planted in the ocean
for the scrupulous love-making of cetaceans
night enclosed
splendid muck heap
where with all its strength with all its wild beasts
the purple muscle of the monkshood of another sun prepares to spring

Mort à l'aube

Lutteur il souffle sur des tisons
son visage mal géré par la nuit
d'où la trompe de ses lèvres siffleuses à serpents
imagine mal un corps torturé dans l'oubli

Homme sombre qu'habite la volonté du feu
quand un viol d'insectes s'éparpille dans sa faim
quand ses pieds diminuent ses orteils en tronçons de vers nus
et que seuls les tisons de ses yeux ont bien pris

Mince tison il est celui qui par toutes les veines du sang
de sa grêle coquille et parmi une forêt qui défiera
le complot d'évêques des latérites porte le saut d'un fût
dans un secret si clair qu'aucun homme ne l'a cru

Death At Dawn

A fighter he blows on his brands
his face mismanaged by the night
from which the horn of his lips hissing serpents
ineptly projects a body tortured in oblivion

Tenebrous man inhabited by the will of the fire
when a rape of insects scatters through his hunger
when his feet diminish his toes into segments of naked worms
and only the brands of his eyes are truly ignited

A thin brand is he who by all the veins of the blood
of his slender shell and in a forest that shall defy
the episcopal plot of laterites carries the leap of a bole
in a secret so transparent that no man believed it

À hurler

Salut oiseaux qui fendez et dispersez le cercle des hérons
et la génuflexion de leur tête de résignation
dans une gaine de mousse blanche

Salut oiseaux qui ouvrez à coups de bec le ventre vrai du marais
et la poitrine du chef du couchant

Salut cri rauque
        torche de résine
        où se brouillent les pistes
        des poux de pluie et les souris blanches

Fou à hurler je vous salue de mes hurlements plus blancs que la mort
fou à hurler mes hurlements à décosser les pépites de neige vierge sont des
diamants plus beaux à découper en franges de drapeau la rouille qui s'empare
de vos charmes
de vos armes

Mon temps viendra que je salue
grand large
simple
où chaque mot chaque geste éclairera
sur ton visage de chèvre blonde
broutant dans la cuve affolante de ma main

Et là là
bonne sangsue
là l'origine des temps
là la fin des temps
là le ruisseau ô chute ô démons ô recours

et la majesté droite de l'œil originel

Howling

Hail birds who cleave and scatter the circle of herons
as well as the genuflection of their resigned heads
in a sheath of white froth

Hail birds who with your beaks rip open the true belly of the swamp and the
chieftain chest of the setting sun

Hail hoarse scream
          resinous torch
          where tracks of rain ticks
          and white mice become blurred

Howling mad I hail you with my howlings whiter than death
howling mad my howlings to shell the nuggets of virgin snow are diamonds
more beautiful for cutting up into flag fringes the rust that seizes hold of
your charms
of your weapons

My time shall come for me to hail
great vast
simple
where each word each gesture shall light up
on your face of a blond goat
grazing in the maddening vat of my hand

And there there
good leech
there the beginning of time
there the end of time
there the runnel oh fall oh demons oh reprieve

and the erect majesty of the original eye

Jugement de la lumière

Fascinant le sang les muscles
dévorant les yeux ce fouillis
chargeant de vérité les éclats routiniers
un jet d'eau de victorieux soleil
par lequel
justice sera faite
et toutes les morgues démises

Les vaisselles les chairs glissent dans l'épaisseur du cou des vagues
les silences par contre ont acquis une pression formidable

Sur un arc de cercle
dans les mouvements publics des rivages
la flamme
est seule et splendide dans son jugement intègre

The Light's Judgment

Captivating the blood the muscles
devouring the eyes this muddle
loading truth onto routine bursts
a water jet of victorious sun
through which
justice shall be done
and all arrogance dismissed

The plates the flesh slide into the thickness of the neck of the waves
silences on the other hand have taken on a terrifying pressure

Over the arc of a circle
in the public movement of shorelines
the flame
is solitary and splendid in its upright judgment

NOTES

For these notes, I have drawn upon Gregson Davis's *Non-Vicious Circle / Twenty Poems of Aimé Césaire* (Stanford: Stanford University Press, 1984); René Hénane's *Glossaire des termes rares dans l'oeuvre d'Aimé Césaire* (Paris: Jean-Michel Place, 2004); Clayton Eshleman and Annette Smith's *Aimé Césaire: The Collected Poetry* (Berkeley: University of California Press, 1983); A. James Arnold's *Modernism & Negritude: The Poetry and Poetics of Aimé Césaire* (Cambridge, Mass.: Harvard University Press, 1981), and other materials. I have also drawn upon information provided to us by Jacqueline Couti, a Martinican who is an assistant professor of French and Francophone Studies at the University of Kentucky, Lexington. When an arcane word can be found in *Webster's Third New International Dictionary*, I have not commented on it here. The collection's title appears to come from the last line of Guillaume Apollinaire's poem "Zone," in his 1913 collection, *Alcools*. Here are the last six lines of the poem:

> Tu marches vers Auteuil tu veux aller chez toi à pied
> Dormir parmi tes fétiches d'Océanie et de Guinée
> Ils sont des Christ d'une autre forme et d'une autre croyance
> Ce sont les Christ inférieurs des obscures espérances
>
> Adieu Adieu
>
> Soleil cou coupé

In Ron Padgett's translation:

> You walk toward Auteuil you want to go home on foot
> To sleep among fetishes from Oceania and Guinea which put
> Christ in another form with other inspirations
> They are inferior Christs of dark aspirations
>
> Goodbye and God keep you
>
> Sun throat cut

Addressing the book's title, which recontextualizes Apollinaire's final line, Gregson Davis writes:

Apollinaire's dawn sun splashing its bloodred colors across the sky shares features of Césaire's many images of violent death and resurrection. An earlier version of Apollinaire's lines provides a further connection with Césaire's themes by linking the sun to violence directed against the poor and outcast: "The sun is there it's a sliced throat / As perhaps one day will suffer some of the poor who I have met / The sun frightens me, it spills its blood all over Paris." Whether or not Césaire knew this version, his commitment to the blacks of colonial Martinique would have led him to identify Apollinaire's assassinated sun of the modern metropolis with oppressed classes and races.

Césaire's "Ode à la Guinée" ("Ode to Guinea") can also be thought of as a response to Apollinaire's lines, rejecting the judgment of the "inferior Christs" in an ode to this mythical African paradise.

It is also perhaps pertinent to point out here that a later poem in this collection, "Cheval" ("Horse"), with its "entangled vipers of my torments," and its repetitional emphases on blood, brings Apollinaire's closure to bear on the myth in which Pegasus, vehicle of poetic inspiration, is released from Medusa's neck as Perseus slices off her serpent-bristling head. One might also detect transformational traces of the Medusa in such lines of "Horse" as: "my blood in which from time to time a woman in solar perfection shoots out all her tuberous stems and vanishes in a tornado born on the far side of the world."

Lastly, Hénane informs us (pp. 45–46) that "cou coupé" is the name of a Senegalese finch (*amadina fasciata*), the cutthroat finch, its white-spotted gray plumage marked by a collarette of red feathers, making it appear to have a slashed throat. According to Hénane, such finches were to be found in Paris in the early years of the twentieth century as exotic caged birds. In 2003, Hénane writes us, he showed Césaire a drawing of the cutthroat finch and the poet told him that he had not known of its existence.

Concerning our translation of the book's title: based on all of the above information, it is clear to us that "cou" should be rendered as "throat," as the action would appear to be that of slashing a throat and releasing a gush of blood that is related to the brightness and force of the sun. While Padgett's rendering of the Apollinaire line ("Sun throat cut") is not inaccurate, in our opinion it feels stiff in English and lacks the sound play of the original, the five vowels making up "Soleil cou coupé." As there is no way to match these sounds in English, we have proposed "Solar Throat Slashed," with two open "o" vowels and a consonant repetition of "r" in the first two words and of "s" in the first and third words.

When Césaire edited the 1948 *Soleil cou coupé* to construct the 1961 *Cadastre*, he eliminated thirty-one poems and cut out material, to varying degrees, in another twenty-nine, leaving only twelve poems untouched. He then added the edited and untouched poems, along with two new poems made up of fragments of eliminated poems, to the ten poems of *Corps perdu* (*Lost Body*—which had been published in 1950 in a limited edition for bibliophiles with thirty-two engravings by Picasso), making up the fifty-three poems of *Cadastre*. In the notes to follow, I provide information concerning which poems were eliminated, what material was cut from the edited poems, and which poems remained unchanged. Readers can compare the translations presented in this book with those in *Cadastre* by referring to pages 162–265 in *The Collected Poetry*, translated by Annette Smith and myself.

Solar Throat Slashed is Aimé Césaire's most fulgurating collection of poetry. Animistically dense, charged with eroticism and blasphemy, and imbued with African and Vodun spirituality, this book takes the French surrealist adventure to new heights and depths. A Césaire poem is a crisscrossing intersection in which metaphoric traceries create historically aware nexuses of thought and experience, jagged solidarity, apocalyptic surgery, and solar dynamite. Facing the locks of the void, Césaire proclaims:

> What have I to discard? Everything by god everything. I am stark naked. I have discarded everything. My genealogy. My widow. My companions. I await the boiling. I await the baptism of sperm. I await the wingbeat of the great seminal albatross supposed to make a new man of me. I await the immense tap, the vertiginous slap that shall consecrate me as a knight of a plutonian order.

The irregular punctuation and a few other possible typesetting oddities in the poems deserve a little commentary. The tendency in the poems is to eliminate punctuation, but there are enough exceptions to this procedure to make us wonder if Césaire himself read and approved the collection's final proofs. Some stanzas end with a period, while others do not. And poems ending with a period often lack periods or other punctuation at the end of interior stanzas. Some poems have no periods in them at any point. "To the Serpent" has twelve interior periods, for example, but no final one. "Permit" has no interior punctuation for its first three stanzas but a period at the end. "Forfeiture" is the only poem in the collection with more or less conventional punctuation throughout. I say "more or less" because there are run-on sentences in the piece that conventionally would have carried commas or dashes. Since we know of no meaningful rationale for standardizing punctuation (or leaving it out completely), we have followed the presentation of the original edition. Our position on this matter is backed up by Daniel Maximin and Gilles Carpentier, the editors of the 1994 *Aimé Césaire: La Poésie*. In that volume they reproduce the erratic punctuation for all the poems in the 1948 *Soleil cou coupé*.

However, in four cases we have decided that printers' errors, beyond simple misspellings, seem to have been involved and so we have made the following changes: In "Attack on Morals," second line, we have presented "time" with a lower case "t" since it appears that way at another point in this poem. In "Several Miles from the Surface" we have lined up the oddly indented ninth line flush left with the rest of the lines. We have done the same thing with the oddly indented penultimate line in "Ex-Voto for a Shipwreck." And in "From a Metamorphosis," while "tsumami" is an acceptable spelling of the word in French, we have changed it in English to "tsunami." Three of these four decisions are supported by Maximin and Carpentier; in the case of the word "time" in "Attack on Morals," they have capitalized it each time that it appears. In the 1948 text, there are a dozen or so instances in which it appears that printer errors resulting in misspellings have occurred. We have indicated these at the end of the notes on individual poems.

Lastly, we also regard the hyphen in *Soleil cou-coupé* on the title page of the original edition as a printer's error. Elsewhere the title always appears without the hyphen.

*

"Magic": No changes.

"The Nubian Vultures Have the Floor": At the end of line 2, "its pomp and its armpits" was cut, as well as "What horrible cocaine. Neither thumb nor screw" in line 6.

"Lynch I": This poem was eliminated.

> murderess-hole: I had originally translated the phrase "meurtrière sommaire" as "summary loophole." While "loophole" is one of "meurtrière's" meanings, here it is general and vague. "Meurtrière" means "murderess" and "murder-hole" (a hole in the battlements of a castle through which defenders could throw noxious substances at attackers). Given the erotic seams in the poem, "murderess" seems quite relevant but if used alone eliminates the equally cogent "murder-hole." We have chosen to coin "murderess-hole" (in the spirit of some of Césaire's coinages) to engage both potential meanings. We have also tightened, as it were, "summary" to "succinct."

"Devourer": This poem was eliminated.

"The Law is Naked": Lines 12–23 were cut, except for "There are no more milking machines for the morning that has yet to rise."

"Rain": This poem was eliminated, except for lines 17, 18, 25, and 26, which became the poem "Pluies" in *Cadastre*.

"Velocity": Line 8 was cut.
   In the 1948 text, in line 9, the "n" in "conservés" was inverted and printed as "u."

"Disaster": This poem was retitled as "Tangible Disaster" in the 1961 edition. In line 2 "mandragora remorse" was cut, as was "mystagogical giant" in line 8.
   The word "strom" appears to be a syncope based on "maelstrom."
   According to Césaire, much of the imagery in this poem is a response to the disaster caused by Mont Pelée's 1902 eruption; therefore our translation of "éclat" as "eruption."

"Secret Society": This poem was eliminated.
   In the 1948 text, in line 1 "lagon" was printed as "lagoon"; in line 3 of the third stanza, the "n" in "convexes" was inverted and printed as "u."

"Nocturnal Crossing": This poem was eliminated.

"Among other Massacres": No changes.

"The Griffin": No changes.

"Redemption": No changes.

"Mississipi": Césaire appears to be using an early spelling of Mississippi possibly based on an early French map when the region was still a French colony.
   In the 1961 edition, the repetition of "Mississipi" at the end of lines in the first, second, and third stanzas has been eliminated.

"Blues": No changes.
   The Spanish word "aguacero" means a brief, sudden shower or downpour.
   In the 1961 edition, "of the Rain" was added to the title.

"The Scapegoat": "crepuscular" in line 8 was cut.
   In line 13, the editors of the 1994 *Aimé Césaire: La Poésie* (Paris: Editions du Seuil) have corrected the 1948 "Arborigène" to "Aborigène" (aborigine), treating it as a typo. With the possibility in mind that Césaire may have been inserting "arbre" ("tree") into the word, we have rendered "Arborigène" as "Arboriginal."

"Transmutation": This poem was eliminated.

"Dwelling 1": This poem was eliminated.

"The Sun's Knife-Stab in the Back of the Surprised Cities": This poem was eliminated.
   vever: In Haitian Vodun, a symbolic design formed on the ground by sprinkling cornmeal or some other powder from the hand at the beginning of a ceremony. It represents a Loa or spirit to be invoked.

"When in the Heat of the Day Naked Monks Descend the Himalayas": This poem was eliminated.

fofa: two possible meanings here. Hénane favors a wild and sexy Portuguese dance. More likely, we think, with the monks in the poem's title in mind, is an Ethiopian hairstyle, short to medium length on the sides or back, with a receding hairline from the forehead back, derived from the style of monks.

"Attack on Morals": This poem was eliminated.

"Son of Thunder": No changes.

In the 1948 text, in line 3, "atolls" was printed as "attolls."

"Permit": This poem was eliminated.

"Solid": This poem was eliminated.

"The Woman and the Flame": This poem was eliminated.

"Millibars of the Storm": The fifth line was cut.

"Gallantry of History": This poem was eliminated.

Ogou: A Vodun Loa who presides over fire, hunting, politics, and war. It is Ogou who is said to have planted the idea, led and given power to the slaves for the Haitian Revolution of 1804.

"Several Miles from the Surface": This poem was eliminated.

"Chevelure": Lines 5–7, 16–25, and 29 were cut.

"Scalp": This poem was eliminated.

"The Tornado": Lines 3–5 were cut.

In line 11, "into a whore's vagina" was cut.

Lines 18–21 were cut.

In line 22, "of the executed" was cut.

"Lynch II": No changes. In the 1961 edition, the "II" in the title was dropped since "Lynch I" was not included in the revised edition.

In the 1948 text, the noun "phosphorescence" was printed with a redundant "phos-" before the line break.

"Apotheosis": This poem was eliminated.

"Crusade of Silence": "Crusade" was turned into a plural for the 1961 edition. In the case of this short poem, instead of listing the cuts and rewrites, we reproduce the translation from *Cadastre* as it appeared in the 1983 *Aimé Césaire / The Collected Poetry*, translated by Annette Smith and myself. The comparison will give the reader of the present volume some insight on the extent to which Césaire eliminated the dense, animistic fervor of much of the writing in the original *Soleil cou coupé*.

Crusades of Silence

And now
that the spacious birds are committing suicide
that the animals' entrails are blackening on the sacrificial knife
that the priests are planting themselves a vocation at
the crossroads knotted in the compost of bric-a-brac

Black it is nonblack black
black locality
locus of stigmata
flesh aflame dimmed remembrance

when in your venisons a stone fills with a thousand faces the huge hole that the dark water of speech made in your flesh

extinct Chimborazo still devours the world

"Totem": No changes.
"Unmaking and Remaking the Sun": This poem was eliminated.
   According to Hénane, "chicken droppings" also refers to the flowers of the garden balsam.
   In the 1948 text, 5 lines from the end, the verb "nais" was printed with an ungrammatical "î."
"Samba": No changes.
   Phoronids are small marine wormlike animals bearing numerous tentacles. Therefore our translation of "queues" as "tentacles."
"Intercessor": No changes, accept for the title change to "Interlude."
   In the 1948 text, the final "s" was missing on the word "entrelacs," line 7.
"The Wheel": No changes.
   In the 1948 text, in line 7, the circumflex accent was omitted from "saoûle."
"Calm": No changes, other than the elimination of the stanza break between lines 15 and 16.
"New Year": The last 6 lines were cut.
"Ex-Voto for a Shipwreck": Nine lines of lines 15–37 were cut and others were reworked; see pp. 176–77 of *The Collected Poetry*.
   Shaka (1781–1828) was a great Zulu military chieftain who between 1818 and 1828 unified the Natal peoples and challenged European settlers in southern Africa.
   In the 1948 text, the hyphen was omitted from "Bonne-Espérance."
"All the Way from Akkad from Elam from Sumer": Lines 1–17 have been reworked (see pp. 194–95 of *The Collected Poetry*).
   The second half of line 14, and lines 15–16, were cut.
   "supernaturally" was cut from line 21.
   Concerning the "Master of the three paths" in the poem: Arnold makes a reasonable case that this master is Legba, the Loa traditionally invoked to open the path between this world and the spirit world, and that the poem "does suggest, with its peculiar use of repetitive invocation, the spiritual or religious aura of a prayer" (*Modernism & Negritude*, p. 221).

"To the Serpent": This poem was eliminated.
>In the 1948 text, in the final line, the article "une" lacked the final "e," marker of the feminine modifier of "main."

"Torture": This poem was eliminated.
>In the 1948 text, 6 lines from the end, "ellipses" was spelled "élipses."

"Pennant": This poem was eliminated.
>Samory Touré (1830–1900), born in what is now Guinea, was a sovereign and a fighter against French colonization in West Africa. His military conquests enabled him to create an empire called Wassoulou that stretched from Guinea to what is now Burkina Faso, covering some 400,000 square kilometers. He was known as "Almamy" ("commander of the believers").

"To Africa": "that will occur in the year 3000" was cut from line 3.
>Lines 22–28 were shortened and turned into three lines (see pp. 196–97 in *The Collected Poetry*).
>
>Line 34 was cut, as well as lines 42–53.
>
>*peasant*: In translating the French "paysan" we considered using the word "farmer" to avoid the sometimes negative connotations of "peasant." However, given the African context of the poem, in which a figure is striking the soil with a "daba" (pick hoe), we decided that "peasant" was more suitable. In responding to our query, our Martinican consultant Jacqueline Couti wrote to us: "If you want to keep 'peasant' it might be useful to remind the reader that this word describes the traditional rural population in pre-industrialized countries. When Césaire uses "paysan" it is a term of endearment praising nature and the traditional way of life not tainted by modernization. Of course those working the land were oppressed but they were more than aware of how useful they were to their country."
>
>In the 1948 text, toward the middle of the poem, "isthmes" was printed as "ithsmes."

"Delicacy of a Mummy": This poem was eliminated.

"Demons": Lines 8 and 9 were shortened into one line.

"Swamp": The first five-line stanza was cut except for the beginning three-quarters of the opening line.
>In line 10, "the victims of" was eliminated.
>
>The stanza break between stanzas 3 and 4 was eliminated.

"Noon Knives": The first long prose stanza was split into two stanzas.
>The stanza break after the new second stanza was taken out.
>
>The original second and third stanzas, totaling forty lines, were reworked into seventeen lines (see pp. 200–201 in *The Collected Poetry*; also, for an interesting commentary on the 1961 editing of "Noon Knives," see Janice Horner Kaufman's article, "Tracing the Paideuma in Aimé Césaire's

Poetry: From *Solar Throat Slashed (Soleil cou coupé)* to *Cadaster (Cadastre)*, New West Indian Guide vol. 77 no. 1 & 2 (2003). Commenting on the poem's opening, Kaufman writes: "This poem specifically evokes the Haitian Revolution of 1804 in the first line: 'When the Niggers make Revolution they begin by uprooting giant trees from the Champ de Mars which they hurl like bayings into the face of the sky.' 'Le Champ de Mars' is the public square in front of the palace in Port-au-Prince." See Arnold's introduction for our justification in translating "Négres" as "Blacks" here.

parachites: In ancient Egypt a class of embalmers whose task, while preparing the mummy, was to make a lateral cut with a silex knife into the cadaver in order to extract the viscera.

"Idyll": This poem was eliminated.

In the 1948 text, toward the middle of the poem, the word "blanche" in the phrase "page blanche" was printed as "blance."

"Password": This poem was eliminated, except for the last seven lines which became the poem "Antipode" in *Cadastre*.

"Turn of Events": This poem was eliminated.

"Preliminary Question": This poem was eliminated.

"Tattooing Gazes": This poem was eliminated.

"At the Locks of the Void": The last three sentences of the first prose stanza were cut.

In stanza 3 (the second prose stanza), "it is a skein of iron for reinforced concrete" was cut from line 24; "it is the graphic representation of a seismic floodtide" was cut from line 26; "I await the baptism of sperm" was cut from line 32; "I await in the depths of my pores the sacred intrusion of the benediction" was cut from line 35.

In stanza 4, lines 39, 40, 42, and 43 were cut.

In stanza 5, line 46 was cut.

In stanza 8 (the last stanza), "Europe," in line 51, has been replaced by "Ancient name," and the last three lines of the poem, "all that is not you / Europe / eminent name of the turd" have been reduced to a single phrase, "considerable hiccup," significantly lessening the poem's original attack on European civilization.

"Forfeiture": This poem was eliminated.

"To the Night": This poem was eliminated.

"Commonplace": Lines 10–15 were cut, as was line 17.

Lines 20–50 have also been cut.

arain: an archaic word in English for "spider" chosen to match the archaic French word "araigne."

"Ode to Guinea": Lines 9–21 and 26–39 were cut.

"Horse": "and sentiments" was cut from line 3.

Lines 10–22 were mainly cut and slightly reworked (see pp. 208–209 in *The Collected Poetry*).

From line 31 "of the furrow" was cut.

"Antipodal Dwelling": This poem was eliminated.

"Sun and Water": Line 12 was cut.

"From a Metamorphosis": This poem was eliminated.

jamblique: According to Hénane, there are two Jambliques or Lamblicuses; one from second-century Syria was the author of a novel, *The Babylonians*; the second was a Neo-Platonic Greek philosopher, who died in 333 C.E. and who was the author of a number of mathematical tracts and a fierce adversary of Christianity.

"March of Perturbations": No changes.

"Barbarity": No changes.

"Non-Vicious Circle": In line 10, the future tense of the verb "sink" was converted into a present tense.

"Different Horizon": In line 7, "another sun" was changed to "our sun."

"Death at Dawn": Line 7 was cut.

In line 9, "by all the veins of the blood" was cut.

"Howling": Lines 11–13 and 24 were cut.

"The Light's Judgment": No changes.

—Clayton Eshleman, January–March 2010

ACKNOWLEDGMENTS

The publisher and translators wish to thank the following magazines and Web sites that have published poems that now appear in this book: *Alligatorzine* (Belgium), *ActionNow, Asymptote,* bookslut.com, *Brooklyn Rail, Catch Up, Denver Quarterly, The Glade of Theoric Ornithic Hermetica, Guernica, House Organ, Jivin' Ladybug, Jubilat, Lana Turner, Mantis, Massachusetts Review, The Nation, New American Writing, Poems & Poetics, The Wolf* (England).

Our gratitude to Eskil Lam for permission to reproduce Wilfredo Lam's painting *Personage* (1973).

ABOUT THE AUTHORS

AIMÉ CÉSAIRE (1913–2008) was best known as the cocreator of the concept of *négritude*. The French government organized a state funeral in Martinique, his island home, in April 2008. In 2011 a plaque in his honor will be sealed in a wall of the Panthéon in the Latin Quarter of Paris, where the French nation commemorates its heroes. A. JAMES ARNOLD is an emeritus professor of French at the University of Virginia. He is the lead editor of Césaire's complete literary works in French (in progress) and author of *Modernism and Negritude: The Poetry and Poetics of Aimé Césaire*. In 1990 he published a substantial essay as the introduction to *Aimé Césaire: Lyric and Dramatic Poetry, 1946–82* (Charlottesville, VA: University Press of Virginia), translated by Clayton Eshleman and Annette Smith. CLAYTON ESHLEMAN is a professor emeritus at Eastern Michigan University and the foremost American translator of Aimé Césaire. He is the author of *The Grindstone of Rapport / A Clayton Eshleman Reader* and translator of *The Complete Poetry of César Vallejo*. In 2001 Wesleyan University Press published a revised edition of Césaire's long poem *Notebook of a Return to the Native Land*, translated by Eshleman and Smith.

Library of Congress Cataloging-in-Publication Data
Cesaire, Aime.
[Soleil cou-coupe. English & French]
Solar throat slashed : the unexpurgated 1948 edition / Aime Cesaire ;
translated and edited by A. James Arnold and Clayton Eshleman.
   p. cm.
Includes bibliographical references.
ISBN 978-0-8195-7070-3 (cloth : alk. paper)
I. Arnold, A. James (Albert James), 1939– II. Eshleman, Clayton. III. Title.
PQ2605.E74S613   2011
841'.914—dc22   2010053421